BUSINESS ENGLISH AND COMMUNICATION

BUSINESS ENGLISH AND COMMUNICATION

Written by
Moira Sambey

Edited by
The Management Development Centre of Hong Kong

The Chinese University Press

The Management Development Centre of Hong Kong

ISBN 962-201-842-4

THE CHINESE UNIVERSITY PRESS
The Chinese University of Hong Kong
Sha Tin, N.T., Hong Kong
Fax: +852 2603 6692
      +852 2603 7355
E-mail: cup@cuhk.edu.hk
Web-site: http://www.cuhk.edu.hk/cupress/w1.htm

Printed in Hong Kong

Contents

Preface

Realizing the need for a management programme for Chinese-speaking managers and supervisors in Hong Kong, The Management Development Centre of Hong Kong developed "The Management Foundation Programme" in 1995. The objectives of the programme are:

1. To equip Hong Kong managers and supervisors with practical management skills.
2. To help graduates to obtain international accreditation of professional bodies.

The programme has a total of eight subjects:

1. Principles of Management
2. Economics for Managers
3. Organizational Behaviour and Personnel Management
4. Management Applications of Quantitative Methods
5. Management Information Systems
6. Hong Kong Business Law
7. Business English and Communication
8. Supervisory Skills

Apart from Business English and Communication, these books are written in Chinese. In July 1994, The Management Foundation Programme was granted equal standing with The Foundation Programme of The Institute of Chartered Secretaries and Administrators (ICSA). Graduates of The Management Foundation Programme can apply for exemption in the ICSA Foundation Programme.

As a course book of The Management Foundation Programme, this book is written in clear, simple English to facilitate understanding. Local exercises and examples are used to reinforce key concepts. Cartoons and illustrations are used to attract the interest of the students while reading.

The manuscript of this book was prepared by Ms. Moira Sambey;

the cartoons were drawn by Ms. Chan Yuk-ying. The manuscript has been edited and proofread by staff of The Management Development Centre of Hong Kong and The Chinese University Press. Without their dedication and commitment, this book would not have been completed on time.

The Management Development Centre
of Hong Kong
October 1998

About the Author

Moira Sambey has been a teacher to adults of English, English as a Foreign/Second Language, and Business English since 1978.

Born in Canada, she grew up in the United Kingdom. Being a keen creative writer, she has held regular workshops for aspiring writers, and both she and her students have won prizes for their work, including, in Hong Kong, The *Hong Kong Standard's* Job Application Competition (1996), and the *South China Morning Post's* Short Story Competition (1997).

She holds a B.A. (Hons.) degree in Psychology, a P.G.C.E. degree in English and a Cambridge R.S.A. qualification in TEF/SL.

She has resided in France and Switzerland and is presently living in Hong Kong with her husband and their three children, where to date she is working on a novel.

Introduction

Give a man a fish and you feed him for a day. Teach him how to fish and you feed him for a lifetime.

— Chinese proverb

This book can be regarded as a "user's manual," with very much a "teach him how to fish" approach. It is particularly suited to Hong Kong Chinese managers and supervisors in management who need to learn the oral and written skills necessary for effective communication in English.

This is a practical manual where the reader learns by doing. There is emphasis on writing skills, since written English is widely used in business and is the most challenging to master. The exercises at the end of each chapter enable the reader to make a thorough review of the material learned, while the practical tasks aim to get the reader working with and writing real-life material as they would in business.

The initial chapters cover the theory and physical mechanics of communication, and revision of English basics. These are followed by the writing skills, methods and techniques, and then some common strategies used in business messages in English.

Finally, listening and speaking skills are covered, which ask the reader to understand that listening is just as important as speaking, and the exercises and tasks serve to reinforce that fact.

This book, then, will put the practice into the hands of the reader, so that upon completion, he or she will be able to consider himself or herself well on the way to being skilled in English business communication.

1

Business Communication and Effective Writing

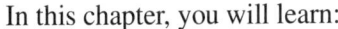

In this chapter, you will learn:
- what communication is;
- how communication works.

If you can take a few minutes to think about business and management, and write down in a list all the things that are necessary to manage a business successfully, you might think that your list would go on forever. Words on your list might be products, services, goods, dates, shipping, factory, manufacturing, time management, accounts, balances, profits, quotas, costs, prices, import tax, sales plans, selling, payment, operations, and many, many more. It is very easy to lose sight of the most important word in any business — *people*. Staff, personnel, workforce, customers — without them, no business would work. And even if all the people were in place, still no business would work if these people did not *communicate* with each other! Can you imagine a business in which no meetings were held, no telephone calls were made, no presentations were given, no faxes or e-mails or voice mails or pager messages or letters or memos were sent, and nobody spoke to each other? Of course not!

Communication between people in business is extremely important for a business to run. The better the communication, the better the business will run.

When you think of communication, perhaps you think of speaking and writing. Communication is indeed speaking and writing, giving a message to the person or people who are listening to you or reading the words that you have written. But communication is also listening and reading, i.e. receiving the message that another person or people are giving to you.

Business communication is sending out and receiving messages in the field of business through speaking, writing, reading and listening.

Almost anyone can speak and listen. But not everyone can speak and listen well. The same is true for reading and writing. Luckily, speaking and listening skills can be improved by anyone, and reading and writing skills can be learned, again, by anyone. The more specialized communication skills needed for business communication can also be learned by anyone, and there is no excuse for not becoming a good communicator both in the business world and in general.

In this chapter we will be looking at communication skills, and why they are important in business. We will also be looking at how communication works — the actual process of sending and receiving messages. We will be taking a look at communication with people from other cultures. Finally, we will see how the four communication skills — speaking, listening, reading and writing — can be developed.

Why Learn to Communicate Well?

If you are in business and/or in management in Hong Kong, you can expect your workplace to be changing rapidly. Many foreign companies have offices in Hong Kong and you may well find yourself dealing with American or Japanese, French or Korean staff. You may travel abroad to other countries on business trips. Good communication is extremely important if your business dealings are to succeed.

In the past ten years, huge steps forward have been made in communication technology. Voice mail, e-mail, the Internet, the fax machine, the pager and the mobile phone are examples, and using these tools as well as possible in business is also important.

Learning to communicate well is the goal of every business executive who wants to aim for the top. The topmost executives have learned that good communication is one of the most important skills to master, and they, like you, had to start somewhere! Like you, as aspiring managers, they started at the beginning. Learning how to communicate well is not difficult, and can be learned by anyone.

Good Communicators — A Valuable Company Asset

Take a look at the classified job advertisements in newspapers. Many, many job advertisements ask for people who are good communicators. Why? Because good communicators are good for business. They bring business to the company. They have learned good people skills, they know how to encourage others to buy and so they can quite easily sell their company's goods and services. Their messages are clear and simple and do not have to be repeated or questioned for meaning. This saves the company time, and, in Hong Kong especially, time is money.

Good communicators can present information well. They know how to present only what is important, and how to present it simply and clearly. Perhaps surprisingly, good communicators are also extremely good listeners. Listening, really listening to people's needs is extremely important in business. A customer who feels that you really listen to him or her will want to do business with you. Good communicators are therefore very valuable to employers and indeed to companies, and companies are always on the search for people with good communication skills.

Many companies give applicants tests which measure their communication skills before deciding on whether or not to employ them. For many companies, good communication skills among its employees is just as important as educational qualifications, if not more so. Interviewing the applicant is the first step for an employer to find out how good his or her communication skills are. At the interview, if you can present ideas well, process information, ask and answer questions, explain yourself and sell yourself, you will have shown to the employer that you are already well on the way to being a good benefit to the company. On top of that, the applicant may be given a written test, and/or perhaps a case to solve, or have a presentation to give, so that the employer will get an all-over idea of the candidate's ability to communicate.

Once you have been recruited, having good communication skills will play a big part in your promotions to top executive positions. Nobody in top management in business is a poor communicator. The higher you climb up the corporate ladder, the more time you will spend on giving and receiving information, which needs excellent communication skills.

Communication in Your Daily Life

Fairly or unfairly, the way we speak and write gives other people a picture of ourselves. People who speak and write well are seen as educated and intelligent and give a good impression. Those who write and speak poorly are held in lower esteem, rightly or wrongly. Learning how to communicate well will give people a good impression of you, in life in general as well as in business.

How Communication Works?

Communication begins with an idea in the mind of the sender. This idea must be expressed, that is, sent out as a message to another person or people. A message can be expressed in words, spoken or written. Speaking is the most common way of expressing an idea.

The person who wants to transmit an idea must be sure to form the idea into a message that the receiver will understand. He or she must choose the words very carefully so that the message will be understood in the way that the sender wants it to be understood. A good communicator aims to make every one of his messages understood exactly as he or she wants them to be understood.

To make sure that the message is understood by the receiver, the sender must choose words and phrases that he knows the receiver will understand. If the words and phrases are not understood, communication breaks down. And usually, when this happens, the relationship between the sender and the receiver dies, either just a little, or completely. Either way, breakdowns in communication are not good for business.

The words the sender chooses to use to express his or her message will depend on several factors. They will depend on the person who is going to receive the message. They will depend on what the sender wants to say and why he or she wants to say it. They will also depend on the sender's communication ability, on the mood of the sender and even on his or her cultural background.

A message does not have to be expressed in words. Nodding or shaking the head in Western cultures gives a message of "I agree" or "I do not agree." Body language sometimes gives very clear messages which do not need words. However, in this chapter, we will be looking at the communication of messages using words. To summarize:

1. Ideas are formed into messages using words.
2. The sender must choose the words very carefully so that he or she can be sure that the receiver will understand the message in exactly the way he or she wants it to be understood.
3. The actual words that the sender chooses to express his or her message depend on several factors.

In order to get a message across to the receiver, the sender needs to find a way to send it. He or she can choose to use the telephone, the fax machine, e-mail, a letter, a memo, a report or a presentation, for example. Whichever way he or she chooses will depend on how important the message is, how much information it contains, how urgent it is, the position of the person who is to receive the message, and even how expensive it would be to send it.

The Person Who Gets Your Message

It is important that your message is received by the receiver in the best conditions. If the message is not clear, if the receiver does not know about the subject or is not interested in the subject of the message, if the receiver does not feel like getting a message at that moment, if the message has poor communication skills, if the receiver has noise and distractions around him or her, then your message will not be well received!

However, if the message is clear, if the receiver knows about the subject and is interested in it, if the receiver is open to receiving a message at that moment, if the message has good communication skills and if the receiver is alone to be able to concentrate on the message, then the message will have the greatest influence on the receiver, because it has been received in the best conditions.

The receiver of your message will usually need to send a reply back to you. This is called "feedback," and feedback is an important part of communication. Imagine having a "conversation" with someone who does not give a reply back to any sentence you say!

Feedback tells the sender that the message was received by the receiver and was understood. (Sometimes feedback tells the sender that the message, although received, was not understood!) The sender can encourage feedback by asking the receiver if there is anything that he or she did not understand in the message, or if anything was not clear. The receiver can demonstrate that he or she has understood the message by repeating it in his or her own words. Some very good communicators, at the end of their message to the receiver, ask the receiver to do a certain job which will show the sender that the receiver has understood the message.

Communication Breakdown

Sometimes communication between the sender and the receiver breaks down, and this can happen for many reasons, and at any stage in the sending or receiving of a message.

Communication breakdown is more likely to happen when the message must be transmitted through several people before it reaches the receiver. The message will be further misunderstood if the feedback also has to travel through several people.

Communicating Globally

Communication breakdown is even more likely when the message must pass between people of different cultures, because different messages (non-verbal or verbal) may mean different things to different people, or it may be that the messages of one culture do not even exist in another. Misunderstandings arise — communication breaks down. But it is very important nowadays to make an effort to master communication between peoples of different cultures. The world is shrinking fast and doing business with people from countries both close to Hong Kong and far away is very likely. The more senior your position is, the more likely it will also be that you will have to travel to foreign countries to deal with people there. If all people in business all over the world try hard to understand each other, communication will be easier and business will be more of a pleasure for all.

You may be curious to know what kind of cultural differences would be a problem for good communication. One example is the basic difference in the way English-speaking Westerners and people from some Asian countries think about the way that running a business or a company should be structured. People who grow up and are educated in Asia learn to value teamwork in the workplace. To them, organizations and groups are important, and it is also important to conform as a group to company policies. Business decisions made by a group, and group agreement, are valued and put into practice. Westerners, on the other hand, place much more value on the independence of the individual, believing that group organization is not the way to progress. Westerners

Words have different meanings when being used differently

believe strongly in individual thought, initiative, action, and responsibility, and have a strong need for freedom to express themselves as individuals. These basic differences can lead to misunderstandings in communication between Asians and Westerners in a business setting, or even result in communication breakdown.

Another example of the way in which communication problems can arise in business is the directness of Westerners contrasted with the more indirectness of Asians. Western people feel that indirectness wastes time and energy — they want to get straight to the point in business negotiations. This attitude may offend people from some Asian countries, who feel that it is rude to speak directly in business issues. Westerners also value direct communication, saying what they mean, and meaning what they say, and are suspicious of people who communicate in roundabout, or, to them, misleading ways. They often do not understand the Asian need to "save face" by sometimes saying yes when they mean no, and from this single issue alone, huge misunderstandings and communication problems very often arise.

Making Communication Easy

As mentioned above, because the business world is shrinking fast, it is very important for people of all countries and cultures to learn how to communicate successfully with each other. Learning to think about different people in a different way is the first step towards successful communication with them. There are three main ways to change the way you think about other people:

Stop Thinking That Your Way Is the Best Way

Unfortunately, many people believe that the way in which their culture behaves is the only right way. These people should try instead to accept that there is no right or wrong way, just different ways. If you expect people to behave as you do, and if other cultures expect you to behave as they do, misunderstandings and communication problems will be the result.

Do Not Judge People or Situations

This means looking at people or situations and accepting them as they are, without wishing that they were different. It means being patient in a situation in which you would normally be annoyed, and being patient without judgement. It means trying to really understand why the other person behaves the way he does, and accepting it.

Realize That All the People in One Culture Do Not Behave in the Same Ways

How would you describe American people? Perhaps your only contact with Americans has been groups of American tourists at the Star Ferry or on the Peak. Perhaps, observing them, you came to the conclusion that they were loud. And your opinion of the Japanese? Strange? Untrustworthy? Easy to fool?

Having opinions like these, which group together all the people of one common culture, is called forming stereotypes of these cultures. In a business setting, it is dangerous to carry your ideas over onto individual people, as these wrong impressions can create misunderstandings and are very unfair. Instead, try to see each person as an individual human being. Remember, you would hate to be stereotyped by somebody else.

Communicating with Culturally Different People

Perhaps you will have business dealings with Japanese, or Korean, or Taiwanese or Thai or French or Spanish people, where English is not the first language of either of you. Of course, business will be much smoother if you can fluently speak the language of the other person, or he or she can fluently speak Cantonese. But if this is not the case, both of you will have to communicate in English. Communication between yourself and the other person will be made easier if you (and, hopefully, the other person!) can remember the following points and put them into practice:

1. Make your English as simple as possible. Keep your vocabulary and sentences very simple.
2. Find out if your listener has understood what you have said by asking him or her to give you feedback, or by asking questions, the answers to which will tell you if your listener had understood you.
3. If you have to explain several points, stop after each point to check if your listener has understood you. Do not give the full explanation and then check for understanding at the end.
4. Speak very clearly, giving your best pronunciation in English. Speaking slowly can help too.
5. If there is a misunderstanding, apologize to the other person for not explaining clearly enough.
6. If your listener understands you, he or she will keep his eyes on yours. If you see that your listener is looking away, it usually means that the understanding of your listener has been lost. If this is the case, stop immediately and go back to where you think you may have lost him or her.
7. Good communication also means listening! To be a good communicator, it is extremely important that you really listen to what the other person is telling you. Listen without interrupting or trying to finish his or her sentences — let him or her finish what he or she wants to say.
8. Give the other person at least as much time to talk as yourself. Talking too much while not letting the other person say much is bad communication; it is also very rude, as it shows a lack of respect for what he or she has to say.

Written Communication

If you have to send a written communication to someone whose first language is not English, many of the points above also apply.

If the written communication is important, for example if you are trying to negotiate a sales deal with the other person, employ a professional translator. Write figures for numbers, instead of spelling them out. Always quote prices in the currency of the other country.

Sometimes, American dollars are used as a standard, but this would not be wise in countries where America is not popular.

For dates, remember that Americans mention the month first, followed by the day. In the United Kingdom and in most other countries of the English-speaking world, the day is followed by the month — however, many countries are aware of the American way and great confusion can be the result. When will the order be shipped if you write 3.2.98? On the third of February or on the second of March?

As a result, it is always better to write the date out in words to avoid confusion.

Getting Better at Communicating

You have seen in this chapter how good communication skills are important. You have learned how communication works between the sender and the receiver. You have understood that good communication is very important in business. In fact, poor communication, resulting in misunderstandings and confusion, can result in lost business, which no company can afford!

Good communicators are made, not born. This means that good communication skills can be learned by anyone, which is good news! To remind you, the four communication skills are speaking and listening, reading and writing, and in all four of these areas you can learn to improve. And, like any other skill, practice makes perfect. The more you practise your communication skills, the better your skills will be.

In this book, you will learn how to develop your communication in all four of these skills. At the end of each chapter you will have exercises and tasks for you to put into practice the ideas you have learned. Sometimes, you will have to really think for yourself, and develop some creative ideas!

Developing Your Communication

How does a carpenter learn his trade? First, he must *get to know the tools* that he is going to use. He must understand how each tool works, and how it can help him in his craft.

Second, he must ***learn the techniques*** that he can use to make each tool work for the best result, how to make each tool give him the best result on the wood.

Third, he needs ***an action plan***, for example if he is to make a chair. What is the best way to make a chair? What way is known by all other carpenters to be the best way?

Finally, the carpenter needs to ***practise and practise*** the three above points, until he is indeed truly a skilled worker with wood.

In the same way, a communicator can develop his art by using the same four steps. The tools of the communicator are the basic units of English — vocabulary, grammar, punctuation, and spelling are some examples. The good communicator has learned how each of his tools works, and knows how each can help him in his craft to communicate well.

The good communicator has learned the techniques of using his tools. He has learned how to use vocabulary, spelling, grammar and punctuation in such a way to give him the best results in his communication.

The good communicator also needs to have an action plan. What are the best-known ways to write a business letter, or give a presentation? What ways do all good communicators know are the best ways?

Finally, the good communicator will have practised, and practised over and over again, the three steps above, making himself into a very effective communicator indeed.

Exercise I

1. Circulate freely in the classroom, introducing yourself to everybody else by giving your name with a big smile, a firm handshake and good eye contact!
2. Write a short paragraph about yourself giving your name, details about what you do in your job, where you were born, your hobbies and interests, any countries you have visited,

your hopes for the future. Find a partner and swop your paragraphs. Read your partner's paragraph and pick out the main
points. Introduce your partner to the rest of the class using his
or her information. Don't read it!

If you make a mistake, your partner is free to correct you!

Example — "This is Ming, he's a Product Manager with
Rotormola, he was born in Hong Kong, he likes tennis and
going to the cinema, he's been to the United States and he
hopes to be a senior manager of Rotormola one day!"

Exercise II

Answer the following questions in full sentences.

1. List the four ways of communicating.
2. Can communication skills be learned?
3. Why is it important to communicate well in business?
4. List 10 ways to send a message.
5. Why do companies want good communicators?
6. What does the choice of words sent in a message depend on?
7. What are the best conditions for a message to be sent?
8. What are the best conditions for a message to be received?
9. What is feedback?
10. How can you be sure that your message has been understood?
11. List some of the reasons why communication can break down.
12. List three ways you can change the way you think about people from other cultures.
13. List as many ways as possible to help communication between culturally different people.
14. What will make you into a perfect communicator?
15. List the four steps a communicator needs to practise to develop his skills.

Task I

Work in pairs. Think of the culturally different people living and working in Hong Kong, for example Americans, Koreans, Japanese, Indians. Using the simple questionnaire below, find two people to interview from one of the cultural groups above. (The consulate of the country is a good place to go, people are usually waiting and are bored.) For excellent results, record what the people tell you. Ask their permission first!

When you have completed your questionnaires, present your findings to the rest of the class. Do the results surprise you? Do they change the way you think about that cultural group? In what way?

Discuss the findings.

Sample questions for questionnaire.

1. Do you work in Hong Kong? (Yes/No)
2. What job do you do?
3. Do you have to communicate with Hong Kong people in your work? (Yes/No)
4. What communication problems do you experience with them?
5. How do you think these communication problems could be improved or solved?

Task II

You have a close friend who tells you that communication is not important in the kind of work you do. Write a paragraph saying what you would reply to him or her to explain that he or she is wrong! Remember to support your ideas with reasons.

2

Use of Words and
Basic Grammar Structure

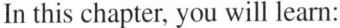

In this chapter, you will learn:
- to make your writing easier to read;
- to use pure English in your writing;
- to develop a strong style in your writing by using words well.

When you speak to people, you do not usually think carefully of the words that you are going to say to them, you just say the words as ideas come into your head.

However, when you write to someone, you will probably agree that you usually spend more time thinking about the words that you are going to write on the paper. This is because you want to make sure that the person who is reading your written communication will understand it. When you are speaking to someone, you can have instant feedback from that person which tells you if he or she has understood your message. If a writer does not make his message clear the first time, the person reading the message cannot ask the writer immediately what he or she means.

It is very important to choose exactly the right words for every written message you send. Even for English-speaking people, the same message can be interpreted differently by different readers. This tells you that you can never be absolutely certain that your message is going to be interpreted the way you want it to be.

But the good news is that you can very much increase your chances of your written message being understood by using the right words and writing techniques. In this chapter, you will learn to use common English words to the best effect. You will also learn not to use words that will not benefit your written communications.

No Place in Business English

You will be glad to know that some forms of English have no place in business communication, and we will be looking at these later. Perhaps you spent much time and effort at school, college or university trying to improve your English by learning and using idioms, clichés, jargon, buzz-words, and slang, thinking that by learning such forms of English you would sound much more like an English speaker. In general speech, yes, the above forms of English would indeed make you sound very much like an English speaker, providing your grammar and pronunciation were good! But these forms of speech are to be avoided in any business communication, and good communicators in business English are always very careful to leave them out. In fact, for the business person whose first language is not English, learning the techniques needed for good speaking and writing is comparatively easy, because the most important rule for the best business communication in English is that your messages should be short and simple, made up of common words familiar to all.

Simple English, Common Words

The first rule about written messages in English is, you will be pleased to know, that it is better to use short, simple, common words instead of long, unfamiliar ones. If you want your business communications to be clearly understood by the people who read them, then write them clearly. This means using words which are familiar to everybody, and this applies to ALL forms of business communications. Here are some long, unfamiliar words which are completely unnecessary in written (and spoken!) business messages. Beside each is the simple, short word which has the same meaning:

- eradicate — get rid of
- nullify — cancel
- operose — difficult
- supposition — idea
- misreckoning — mistake
- missive — letter
- melioration — improvement
- arrears — debt
- placate — please
- adumbration — similarity
- ingress — entrance

Unless you buy *The Times* newspaper, and attempt its crossword every week, you have no business to be learning words like those in the left column. Put your time and energy into learning precise forms of simple verbs, nouns and adjectives instead. We will be looking at these later.

Good communicators use simple English in their written messages.

Try to forget the idea that big, long words are better than simple, short ones. Nothing could be further from the truth. Simple, clear English which is easily understood is what is needed in all business messages. Long, difficult words show disrespect for the reader, and should be avoided. Some writers use long words and complicated sentences to try to impress their readers, especially writers of some legal or government documents. But this style of writing is not impressive, it is ridiculous. Use simple words which everybody understands, every time.

Vocabulary and Grammar

Vocabulary and grammar are two of your most basic and most important tools. It is absolutely essential that your grammar in English is perfect if you want to communicate in English effectively. You should understand how each tense is structured, and how and when it should be used. English grammar is not difficult to learn, and there is no excuse for not mastering it. This is not a grammar book, but it will outline the points that you do need to know. Find a good book on English grammar, (two good ones are *A Practical English Grammar*, written by A. J. Thomson and A. V. Martinet, published by Oxford University Press and *Practical English Usage* by Michael Swan, also published by Oxford University Press) and learn by heart the formats of the irregular verbs, and how the tenses go. You also need to understand how and where to use each tense.

You need to know how to (1) make affirmative statements, (2) make negative statements, (3) ask questions, and negative questions, and (4) form the question-tag question, both positive and negative, *with all tenses*.

For example, here is the simple present tense, showing all four forms. However, isolated sentences do not often give the full idea of how to use the verb. Only a good grammar book and lots of practice will do that! You need to be able to use these four forms with *all* tenses in English.

✍️

I send a fax every day.
I don't send a fax every day.
Do you send a fax every day?
Don't you send a fax every day?
You send a fax every day, don't you?
You don't send a fax every day, do you?

Mastering English tenses, and knowing when to use them, is important in the development of your communication skills. As mentioned above, a good grammar book will be of great use to you.

Remember: good grammar is one of your most important tools in business and management.

Vocabulary

Vocabulary, like grammar, is an extremely important tool. A large vocabulary will help you to find the exact word you want to express your ideas. Think back to the example of the carpenter in the last chapter. The more tools he has, the easier it is for him to make exactly what he wants. So it is with words — the more words you have, the easier it will be for you to express exactly what you want. However, there is no need for you to learn an English dictionary by heart! In fact, it is completely useless to try to learn isolated, individual words. Words must be learned through reading, and it is best if you can learn words which are found in reading which interests you, as research has found that such words are more easily learned.

A good start would be for you to buy an English-language newspaper every week. Find an article which interests you, preferably in the business section, not too long at first. Read it through once, and then again, this time noting any words unknown or little-known to you, and any tenses of any verbs which you are not 100% familiar with. Highlight these with a marker on the second reading. Next, read the article a third time, this time looking up the unknown words in a dictionary. Read them again in the context of the article, noting in your head the sentence in which they appear, and how they are used. Try to memorize it — looking at and thinking about the sentence containing the word will help you to learn it.

Learn to Use Precise Words of Action

English is a very rich language. This means that English words have many shades of meaning. For example, here is a simple English sentence — "the boy looked at the girl."

But in English, there are many words which mean "looked at," and if we put each one instead into the sentence, we have a much more precise idea of exactly how the boy looked at the girl. For example, we can say that the boy stared at the girl, or glanced at the girl, or peeped at the girl, or gazed at the girl, or gaped at the girl, or gawked at the girl, or ogled at the girl, or watched the girl, or observed the girl, or viewed the girl, or spied the girl. All different ways of looking, with a different set of actions behind each one, giving the reader or the listener a very different picture in his or her head!

It's the same with verbs in business communication, and by choosing strong, precise verbs over vague, general verbs, your business messages, spoken and written, will be so much more clear and precise. Action words (verbs) give power and drive to sentences.

Choose your verbs carefully, so that the reader of your messages or the person listening to you can picture in his or her mind what you are saying. Using precise verbs in English is very important, as it makes your message to the reader or the listener very clear and precise, and misunderstandings will not occur.

Look at these examples:

1. I will contact you next week.
2. He said that the shipment would arrive tomorrow.
3. We have thought about the proposal.
4. We are travelling to Japan next month.
5. The last order went out at 5 o'clock.
6. The engineers are going to China tomorrow.
7. We talked to the manufacturers about the problem.

See how much more powerful these sentences sound with more precise verbs:

1. I will telephone you next week.
2. He confirmed that the shipment would arrive tomorrow.
3. We have considered the proposal.
4. We are flying to Japan next month.
5. The last order exited at 5 o'clock.
6. The engineers are flying to China tomorrow.
7. We consulted with the manufacturers about the problem.

Look at the following sentences. Can you tell which are more powerful? Which ones send the message across more forcefully?

He made a suggestion to the Chairman.	He suggested to the Chairman.
She made the recommendation of retrenching four members of staff.	She recommended retrenching four members of staff.
He gave a presentation of the sales plan.	He presented the sales plan.
We put in an order of 500 pieces.	We ordered 500 pieces.
I put forward a proposal about a cutback.	I proposed a cutback.

If you think that the sentences on the right are more powerful, you are right. The sentences on the left present the verbs on the right in their noun forms, making them weaker, less forceful. Where possible, always use strong, powerful action words in short, simple sentences.

Use active verbs in your sentences

Learn to Use Precise Nouns

Do you have a computer, or do you have a Power Macintosh? Do you own a car, or do you own a Mercedes 125? Did you meet a customer, or did you meet Mr. Matsuta Yamamoto? Did you travel to Japan, or did you travel to Sapporo, in Hokkaido? Did you order products, or did you order 200,000 PCB pieces in the ABC line? Did you write a report on the results, or did you write a report on the results of the meeting between Mr. Yamamoto and yourself to discuss the PCB proposal?

You can see how much more informative the second sentences are.

This is because they use precise nouns. A noun is simply a naming word, like computer, car, customer, product, report. But these nouns are not precise. Precise nouns tell what kind of computer, what kind of car, what kind of customer, the name of the place, the name of the product, the name of the person and what kind of report. Using precise nouns in business is extremely important, because it tells the reader or your listener exactly what it is that you are referring to, and misunderstandings will not occur. Remember, we are aiming to use clear, precise English.

Learn to Describe Nouns Precisely

Words that describe nouns are called adjectives. Like nouns and verbs, the adjectives you use in your business communications must also be precise. Don't say that you wrote "a long report."

The adjective here, "long," is not precise. It does not tell the reader or the listener how long the report was. It is much better to say that you wrote "a double-sided, 7-page report." Here, "double-sided" and "7-page" are precise adjectives describing the report.

Similarly, avoid the words "good" and "nice" which are used to death in English! "It was a good meeting" can easily become "it was a productive meeting" and "he gave us a good quote" can also easily become "he gave us a favourable quote."

Never stop trying to think of more precise nouns, verbs and adjectives in your business messages, most especially in your written ones. In meetings, try also to use them, most especially if you are in meetings with people of other nationalities and cultures, although it is harder to think of them as you are speaking. However, with the learning of the necessary vocabulary and lots of practice, even this skill will come easily to you in time.

When to Use Jargon

Jargon is the special words used when talking or writing about a specialized subject. Computer experts in particular have their own jargon, a whole set of vocabulary designed to communicate about computers and everything to do with them. Listening to two computer experts, a person with no interest in computers would not be able to understand much. Similarly, scuba divers, for example, have their own set of jargon related to scuba diving. Likewise, electronics engineers have their own jargon related to the field of electronic engineering.

Using jargon in your writing is fine if you are writing to a person whose knowledge about your subject is equal to or more than yours. If you are a computer engineer, it is acceptable to use jargon when sending a written message to another computer engineer. It is not acceptable to use jargon in your communication if your message is going to be read by a potential customer with little or no knowledge about the engineering of your product. You must be absolutely certain that your reader will understand your jargon if you use it.

Avoid Using Slang

Slang is almost in the same category as jargon. Jargon, as explained above, is acceptable in special cases. The same cannot be said of slang, which has no place in business. Perhaps you have heard the following expressions:

He has it made. (Everything is going perfectly in his favour.)
He has his ass in a sling, now that the boss knows. (He's in deep trouble.)
Get a load of this! (Look at this!)
Our competitor is a dead duck. (In a bad situation.)
He's in the soup/the doghouse now. (In trouble.)
She's got a screw loose. (She's crazy.)
Let's go for broke with this deal. (Risk everything on one big effort.)
I think we should cop out on this customer. (Avoid committing ourselves.)
The new sales representative is such a bonehead. (Stupid person.)

In English, there are thousands of slang expressions. If you have not heard of one or more of the sample above, then imagine how you would feel sitting in a meeting where slang expressions were commonly used, or receiving written communications where slang was usual. For this reason, slang has no place in business communication whatsoever, most especially if you are communicating with people from another country and culture whose first language is not English and who would not understand these expressions at all. At the bar after business, maybe, but keep slang out of any spoken or written business messages. Don't use it.

Avoid Using Idioms

Again, as with slang, idioms have no place in business English. Examples of idioms are:

It's raining cats and dogs. (Raining very heavily.)
He was left holding the bag. (Left to deal with a bad situation.)
We must leave no stone unturned. (Search thoroughly.)
The customer kicked up a fuss. (Complained.)
He held his own in the meeting. (Did very well in a difficult situation with no help.)
Once in a blue moon. (Extremely rarely.)
On a shoestring. (On a very small budget.)
On easy street. (Rich.)
That company is riding high. (Doing well and enjoying it.)
Through thick and thin. (Through bad and good times.)
They're currying favour. (Being nice to someone in order to ask a favour later.)
Not our cup of tea. (Not what we like.)
The company's in the red. (Has lost money, is unprofitable.)

Again, there are thousands in English. And again, for the same reasons that you should not use slang, idioms are not for business communications. In general conversation outside business hours, perhaps, but then only if you know when and where to use them properly!

Avoid Using Clichés

Clichés are expressions which native English speakers have used too much for too long, and now they are old and tired. Some examples are:

last but not least
first and foremost
easier said than done

none the worse for wear
first come, first served

Again, they have no place in business English. Others whose first language is not English may not understand, and besides, we are all so very tired of them!

Avoid Using Buzz-words

A buzz-word is a word currently in fashion. Among teenagers, the current buzz-words (January 1998) are "cool," "evil," "awesome," "real," "wizard." (All used to mean "excellent"!)

A common buzz-word in business now is "logistics." Others are "downsizing," "BPR"' (Business Process Re-engineering), "TQM" (Total Quality Management), "core competence," and "positioning."

Again, avoid them in business communications. They, like clichés, are overused, and others may not understand them.

Don't Repeat Words

Read the following sentences:

1. All employees are asked not to use the employees' restrooms during employees' morning breaks.
2. The customer has said that, as our customer, he would be happy to continue giving us his custom if we give him preferred customer status.

Do you see anything wrong with them? Of course! Words are unnecessarily repeated. As you can see, this makes the sentences difficult to understand and even rather silly.

In your communications, do not repeat words! Can you rewrite the above two sentences in a better way? Here they are as shorter, simpler, more precise messages:

1. All employees are asked not to use their restrooms during their morning breaks.

2. The client has said that he would be happy to enjoy preferred customer status.

A Note on Prepositions

afraid **of** speaking in public
agree **to** (do) something
agree **with** a person
angry **at** something
angry **with** someone
apologize **for** a mistake
apologize **to** a person
arrive **at** a place
arrive **in** a country/city
feel **like** resigning
fly **to** a place
get used **to** working under pressure
in spite **of** the downturn
insist **on** paying
interested **in** the proposal
make a point **of** saying
no point **in** negotiating further
send **to** someone
succeed **in** doing something
suggest **to** someone
what's the point **of** that?

Some verbs in English take prepositions. Some examples are shown above. It is important that you learn the correct preposition that goes with each verb — don't get it wrong!

Exercise I

A   In the sentences below, change the weak, underlined nouns into precise ones. Rewrite the sentences in full.

1. He saw the man yesterday.
2. She ordered 20,000 of their products.
3. The woman said she would contact you on Tuesday.
4. We've just ordered 16 new computers for the Hong Kong office.
5. The boss has just bought another car.
6. This document is very important.
7. The order will arrive on Wednesday.
8. The staff held a meeting.
9. The Chairperson signed the paper.
10. This is the most important thing.

B In the sentences below, add at the * strong, precise adjectives to describe the nouns. Write each sentence out in full.

1. We had a * meeting.
2. The sales executive gave a * presentation.
3. It was a * quota.
4. The Chairman gave a * speech.
5. He is a very * manager.
6. In China there is a * manufacturing plant.
7. The * report was interesting.
8. This * computer can do many things.
9. The * suppliers are always on time.

C The following sentences have words repeated unnecessarily. Rewrite each sentence so that it is shorter and precise.

1. The supplier said that he would supply to us, as our supplier, our order of 20,000 pieces which will be supplied next week.
2. The sales managers held a sales meeting to talk about the present sales plan, focusing on the current month's sales to Japan.
3. Our junior managers attended a management seminar on management skills in Hong Kong, followed by a short in-service management training for junior managers.

4. The company's sales engineers will be flying to China with our sales managers to attend the sales presentation which is to be given by our top sales executive.

5. The customer has complained about our products and our sales engineers will be talking to the customer today about the problem with the products — if necessary the customer will have to use a different product of ours in his products.

D In the following sentences, supply the correct preposition after the verbs. Write each sentence in full.

1. The boss was very angry * the junior secretary.
2. I'm sending this parcel * Tokyo by Fedex.
3. It will arrive * Tokyo tomorrow.
4. It should arrive * his office in the morning.
5. I want to apologize * my mistake.
6. He insisted * paying for the meal.
7. The customer was interested * the proposal.
8. I suggested * him to cancel the meeting.
9. There is no point * signing anything.
10. The senior sales manager made a point * telling us the news.

Exercise II

A In the following sentences, change the underlined verbs into more forceful, precise verbs. Rewrite the sentences in full.

1. We went to see the customer in Taiwan.
2. The supplier said the order would be ready next Monday.
3. He said he would contact us soon.
4. I got his e-mail this morning.
5. They gave us a fair quote.
6. The boss said that we would all get a raise.
7. The buyer thought about the proposal.
8. The speech was well said.

9. The products came on time.
10. He'll go back to Japan next month.

B   **In the following sentences, change the underlined nouns into the more forceful, powerful verb form. Write the sentences out in full. You may have to further change or finish the sentences in your own words.**

1. I gave a presentation to the sales team.
2. I made a suggestion to the boss.
3. The sales manager put forward a proposal.
4. The customer gave a positive reaction.
5. She made a suggestion about reducing the staff.
6. They made a proposition to the supplier.
7. He put forward an announcement that he was leaving the company.
8. He made a statement about the closure of the company.
9. He made an attack on his competitor in the press.
10. He was a witness to the disagreement.

Task

1. Work in pairs. Find a short article in the business section of any English-language newspaper. Is it as clear, simple and precise as you think it should be? Where could it be expressed better (i.e., in a more clear, simple, precise way)? Together, rewrite it in more clear, simple, precise English. Use a dictionary if necessary. Each pair is to use the same (photocopied) article. Discuss your results with another pair.
2. In pairs, think of 3 examples of slang, 3 examples of idioms, 3 examples of clichés and 3 examples of buzz-words in Cantonese. If you were to translate these expressions literally to

two Americans, would they understand? Discuss your findings with another pair.

Would it be fair to use these expressions with foreigners
who understood a minimum of Cantonese? Why/why not?

3

Putting Your Sentences Together for Effective Communication

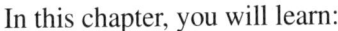

In this chapter, you will learn:
- to write sentences correctly;
- to make important ideas clear in your sentences;
- to balance your sentences;
- to use active and passive verbs;
- to unify your sentences and paragraphs.

As we have seen, good writers know how to use grammar accurately and vocabulary precisely to express exactly what they want to say. But that is not all. Good writers also know how to make sentences work for them. They have learned how sentences are structured and how they can fit together. They know how to change the length of their sentences in a message and how to make their sentences balance to make their written communications more effective. Again, this is something that anyone can learn!

What Are Sentences Made Of?

Sentences are made of components called phrases and clauses. A phrase does not make sense if it stands alone. Here are three examples of phrases:

1. after the meeting

2. by DHL
3. within the hour

There are two types of clauses, dependent and independent clauses.

A clause may make sense if it stands alone, depending on whether it is a dependent or an independent clause. We will look at these below. Let's begin by taking a sentence apart and having a look at the parts.

Read the following sentence:

After the meeting/ we decided to send the document/ by DHL/ within the hour.

In this sentence, there are 3 phrases — "after the meeting," "by DHL," and, "within the hour." "We decided to send the document" is a clause. A clause is a group of related words containing a subject and a verb.

For an example of a dependent clause, look at this sentence:

Send the document by DHL if you are able to do so.

"If you are able to do so" is a dependent clause. It depends on the independent clause in the sentence ("Send the document by DHL"), because it does not make sense by itself if it stands alone.

If you can understand the difference between phrases and clauses, you will be able to write more clearly, without mistakes in your sentences.

In English, the most common faults in writing sentences are:

1. writing fragments;
2. writing run-on sentences;
3. putting commas in the wrong place.

Correcting Fragments and Run-on Sentences

Study these groups of words.

Last month the executive travelled around China.
The whole country.
He visited many customers they placed significant orders.

Which group of words is a proper sentence? What is wrong with the other two groups of words?

A sentence can stand alone and make sense — it expresses a complete thought. If a group of words does not express a complete thought, it is called a fragment. To avoid writing fragments, you must supply the missing words. Look at this group of words:

Left on 2 May.

Notice that the words above tell what happened. They do not, however, tell who or what left on 2 May. What words would make this fragment a complete sentence?

A group of words that expresses more than one complete thought without proper punctuation is called a run-on sentence. Look at the run-on sentence below:

He returned on 29 May he had to write a detailed report.

There are really two complete thoughts here. What are they?

The above group of words has too much information for just one sentence. You could improve it by writing separate sentences, or by joining them together in another way.

Avoid run-on sentences

He returned on 29 May. He had to write a detailed report.
He returned on 29 May, and he had to write a detailed report.
He returned on 29 May; he had to write a detailed report.

Note that run-on sentences cannot be separated by a comma. But this is a very common mistake in English and is the third most common fault in writing sentences. Run-on sentences can be separated with a semi-colon (;), but not a comma!

Sentence Length

When you communicate in writing in English, it is important to vary the lengths of your sentences. Messages which contain sentences of all the same length are very dull to read. Also, messages in which all the sentences are the same length make the reader notice the dullness of the sentences, not the message they are giving!

Look at the following two messages:

(a) *Thank you for your interest in our products. You will be very pleased with them. The XJ8 component should match your BTZ perfectly. We are looking forward to your order. We can ship before the 31st of March.*

(b) *Thank you for your interest in our products. You will be very pleased with them; the XJ8 component should match your BTZ perfectly. We are looking forward to your order and can confirm shipment before the 31st of March.*

You will see that sentence (b) is a better expression of the message than sentence (a). This is because the lengths of the sentences in sentence (b) are different, making the message more interesting to read and also creating more of a "flow."

You may be thinking, "yes, but previously, I learned that short, simple sentences are better than long ones!"

Yes, in general, this is very true, especially if your written messages and communications are directed at people whose first language is not English. Short sentences are more easily understood. But this does not mean to say that all your sentences should be short and simple, especially if your written communications are for native English speakers! (If every sentence in this book were the same length, you would have fallen asleep a long time ago!)

Look at the data in the following table:

Percentage of native English speakers who understand on 1st reading	Length of sentence
100%	1–8 words
90%	9–15 words
80%	16–19 words
50%	20–28 words
30%	29–40 words

In English, the average sentence is between 12 and 15 words long. This does not mean that all sentences should be 12–15 words long, however! Good paragraphs contain sentences of different lengths, some short, some longer.

Emphasizing Important Information

In business communications, you will very often have to send important information. When you are speaking, and you have something important to say, you will probably change your speech pattern so that it is slower. You may make your words clearer by pronouncing them more carefully. Or you may make your voice louder to emphasize important information, or even thump a table to make an important point.

But when you are writing, you cannot use any of these methods to emphasize important points. Of course, if you have a reader, instead of a listener, you want to make sure that your reader knows that some points you want to make are important. To do this, you will have to make your important points very clear and readable, and you will have to make them stand out for the reader.

You can do this in several ways:

1. Underline the important point.
2. **Use boldface to show importance**.

3. USE CAPITAL LETTERS TO SHOW IMPORTANCE.
4. **A COMBINATION OF ALL THREE POINTS ABOVE**
5. Putting the important point between dashes — like this — also makes it stand out.
6. Put items in a list:
    a. First
    b. Second
    c. Third

Other ways to make important points stand out on the page is to use boxes, titles, columns, rows etc. This is particularly effective if done using a computer.

You can also emphasize important points in a written business communication by your writing style. As we saw in a previous chapter, using precise verbs and nouns and using vivid adjectives all help to make important points very clear. Another way to make important information stand out is to mention it first in your message.

The usual way to do this is as follows:

✍

Dear Mr. Yamamoto,

Re: SHIPMENT OF YOUR ORDER OF 120,000 PIECES

We confirm that we will be delivering your order on 24th May. Please note that the 25th and 26th of May are public holidays in the U.S. We will resume business on 27th May; please confirm receipt of your order after then.

"Re" stands for "regarding" (meaning "about" a subject).

Communicating Bad News

You have learned how to emphasize important information by using strong verbs, nouns and adjectives. To communicate bad news, the opposite style is used. General, not precise, words help to soften an unpleasant communication.

Look at the following two sentences.

I regret to tell you that we have to fire you.
I regret to tell you that your services are no longer necessary.

And again:

We are sorry to tell you that your order has been lost.
We are sorry to tell you that we cannot locate your order.

You will see that in the second examples, the unpleasant communications have been greatly softened by the use of general, and not precise words.

Another way of communicating bad news (negative) is to put good news first (positive), followed by the bad — this softens it for the reader. Usually the bad news is put in a dependent clause:

We are presently dealing with a matching volume order for you as we cannot locate your original order.

Sentence Flow

You will understand the importance of writing down sentences in a business communication (or any communication!) in a logical sequence of thoughts. If you have a thought, and write it down, then have another thought which does not follow on from the first thought, and you write it down, then a third thought, which follows on from the first thought but not the second, and write that down too, then have another thought, which follows on from the third thought but not the first or second, the result is a piece of writing which lacks **unity** and **flow**.

It is important that the reader understands that each thought follows on from the one before.

Look at the following sentence:

We are really very sorry that you found our products unsatisfactory. We will be shipping the new BCP pieces to you on the 17th. We hope that you will be happy with this arrangement. We will cover shipping costs of both these and the new products. Our sales engineers are confident that our new BCP components will be more compatible with your product.

Does this message make sense to you? It shouldn't, simply because the writer wrote thoughts down as they came into his head, instead of thinking them out in an ordered sequence before putting them on paper.

Unclear and confused writing also results when phrases and clauses are not kept close to the words that they are describing. Here are some examples:

All office tables will be discounted to customers with metal legs.

Components will be delivered next month to customers with a long shelf life.

Staff must keep toilets clean with a toilet key.

Can you correct them? You will understand why it is important to keep clauses and phrases close to the words they are describing, especially if you are communicating with people who are not native English speakers! Be careful when you are writing, and avoid these kinds of mistakes.

Balancing Your Sentences

Sentences in English are a little like mathematical equations — they must "balance." Balanced sentences help your reader understand what you mean. Here is an example of a sentence which is *not* balanced:

This message is intended for sales executives, sales representatives, sales managers and everybody in the PR department.

You will see that the phrase, "everybody in the PR department," does not balance with the first part of the sentence. The reader is not expecting it. The reader expects the mention of some other people connected with sales to end the sentence. To correct this communication, it would be better to put a full stop after "managers" and create a second sentence, as shown below:

This message is intended for sales executives, representatives and managers. Everybody in the PR department is also expected to attend.

Here is another example of a sentence which is not balanced:

Our goals this month are to increase productivity, to reduce costs, to eliminate time wastage and the employing of two more people.

Again, the phrase, "the employing of two more people," makes the sentence unbalanced. To correct this message, this phrase has to be changed to fit the format of the others.

Our goals this month are to increase productivity, to reduce costs, to eliminate time wastage and to increase employment.

Active and Passive Verb Forms

Look at the following verb forms.

We can do it.	It can be done.
They delivered it.	It was delivered.
I send it daily by Fedex.	It is sent daily by Fedex.
He is doing it.	It is being done.
They will ship it.	It will be shipped.
I was doing it.	It was being done.
They had sent it.	It had been sent.
We could do it.	It could be done.
We should do it.	It should be done.
We would do it.	It would be done.
He could have done it.	It could have been done.
They should have done it.	It should have been done.
She would have done it.	It would have been done.

The sentences on the left are in the ***active voice*** in English. This means that the subject is doing the action.

The sentences on the right are written in what is called the ***passive voice***. This means that the subject is acted upon.

In business communication, the active voice is preferred. However, you will find that the passive voice is in fact used very much in business messages, both spoken and written, and you must learn not only to recognize but also to use the passive voice of all tenses, as in the list above.

The passive voice is especially useful in business in four ways:

1. To make an action stand out — "the message *was noted*."
2. To make the receiver of the action stand out — "*he was voted* sales executive of the year."
3. To soften bad news — "your order *has been cancelled*."
4. To take the blame away from any one person — "your order *has been mislaid*."

Organizing Your Writing

Paragraphs

A paragraph is a group of sentences which develop a main idea. The main idea is usually expressed by the very first sentence in the paragraph. This is called the topic sentence. All the other sentences in the paragraph must relate to the topic sentence and expand it in some way. This is known as ***deductive sentence organization***.

You have learned that sentences follow in a logical, ordered sequence. Paragraphs do the same. Any sentence which supports a new or a different idea should belong in another paragraph, or be changed to support the main idea of the original paragraph.

Read this paragraph:

Fifty years ago, business was nothing like it is today. There were no computers in those days, and air travel was rare. Methods of communication were slow and limited; the telephone, the mailed letter and the telegram were the chief ways of communicating in business. Trying to imagine doing business today without computers, e-mail or fax machines is very difficult!

The first sentence in the above paragraph ("Fifty years ago, business was nothing like it is today.") is the topic sentence, as it expresses the main idea. You will see how the other sentences in the paragraph support and expand this main idea. These other supporting sentences are called *detail sentences*. A paragraph and all its supporting detail sentences are what hold the paragraph together and give it unity. Remember what you learned about sentence unity and flow. The detail sentences in a paragraph must follow a logical order, each following on from the last.

The last sentence in a paragraph may simply supply the last detail, or it may sum up the paragraph so that the reader knows that it is over. When you have written the last detail sentence in one paragraph, you must begin a new paragraph to present your next main idea.

Holding the Paragraph Together

Good writers develop their detail sentences in such a way as to create unity and flow through the paragraph. When all the detail sentences support the topic sentence and *when the detail sentences have flow, the paragraph will hold together*.

There are techniques that can be learned which develop unity in paragraphs through creating unity in the detail sentences.

To develop unity among the detail sentences:

A. Repeat important ideas or words from one sentence to another

Repeating an important idea or word from one sentence in a new sentence helps to bring the reader from one thought to the next. Although you have learned not to repeat words, it is acceptable to do so *in certain circumstances*, especially in different sentences, to reinforce a point. Look at the example below:

The customer has strongly stated that he does not want us to recommend our PX876 components in the future. Because of this, it is important to remind all our Sales Executives not to recommend the PX876 range to him.

In this situation, the important idea is repeated, creating unity between the two sentences.

B. Use pronouns

Using pronouns also creates a sense of unity between sentences.

They are used to join the thoughts in one sentence to the thoughts in the last sentence. Here is an example:

There was a strike by dock workers in Vancouver. **That** resulted in a six-week delay in the delivery of the order.

You can also use the pronouns "this," "they," "these," and "those," the same way.

But be careful when you are using pronouns; you must make sure that your reader understands exactly what the pronoun is referring to. Look at the following sentence.

The customer was given the choice of a full cash refund or a credit voucher. This was issued at his request.

In the above sentence, the reader does not know whether the customer was issued with the cash or the voucher. Reading such sentences is very annoying. Be careful not to write them.

C. Use transitional words and expressions

One of the best ways to achieve unity in detail sentences, and therefore unity in paragraphs, is to use transitional words and expressions. These are phrases which lead one sentence onto the next one, and so give flow to the sentences and thus the paragraph.

Some of the most common transitional words and expressions are:

- however
- as a result
- therefore
- thus
- for this reason

- on the other hand
- moreover
- furthermore
- in this way
- for example
- first
- next
- then
- after that
- finally

Using such transitional words and expressions correctly will greatly help to achieve paragraph unity, as the detail sentences supporting the main ideas will themselves be more unified.

Length of Paragraphs

How do you feel when faced with a long, long paragraph? Discouraged? If so, you're in good company. Most people find short paragraphs much more inviting. For this reason, try to keep your paragraphs short when writing business communications. After all, you don't want your reader to want to avoid reading what you have written!

In business letters in particular, the opening and closing (first and last) paragraphs can be very short indeed. The length of paragraphs in other business document should average between six and ten typed lines.

Organizing Your Paragraphs

We looked at deductive sentence organization above. You may remember that deductive sentence organization is where the main idea is expressed in the first sentence of a paragraph (the topic sentence), followed by several detail sentences which support and expand this main idea.

Another way to organize paragraphs is by using ***inductive sentence organization***. Inductive sentence organization is where examples and reasons are given in sentences, and a conclusion is formed at the end. The following paragraph is an example of inductive sentence organization:

✍

John communicates well with people and really listens to customers' needs. He has a great belief in his products. As a result, he always achieves his sales targets. John is a highly effective Sales Executive.

You will see how the first two sentences simply give information about John. The final sentence draws a conclusion about John, based on the information in the first sentences. In fact, the last sentence is actually the topic sentence, concluded at the end.

Inductive sentence organization is especially useful for communicating bad news (the bad news comes last) or when you want to persuade someone about something (you are building up to make a point). Imagine that you want to borrow some money from a relative. Would you ask for the money first, or would you state all the reasons why you need the money, and then ask for it? Sometimes, putting the big idea last works much better!

Most business communication uses deductive sentence organization, where the main idea is mentioned first in a topic sentence, followed by several supporting detail sentences. However, when you want to deliver an unpleasant communication, or use persuasion, the inductive approach works much better. You will learn more about deductive and inductive sentence organization in a future chapter.

P.O.W.E.R. — The Key to Good Writing!

We have looked at using words effectively, and developing unity and flow through sentences and paragraphs. Now it is time to take a look at the whole writing process. Skilled business communicators use P.O.W.E.R. in all of their messages. P.O.W.E.R. stands for *Planning*, *Organizing*, *Writing*, *Editing* and *Reviewing*. Here are the details of each:

Planning

Every well-written business communication begins with a plan.

1. Think about why you are writing the message.
2. Think about who your reader(s) will be, and try to imagine the reaction they will have to your message.
3. Think what you want to achieve by sending the message.
4. Think of how you are going to send your message (fax? e-mail? telephone?) and what feedback you expect.
5. Decide what ideas you would like to develop, and what you are going to emphasize and de-emphasize.

This planning is necessary whether you are giving feedback to another person's message or sending out a message of your own.

Organizing

The next step is organizing the message. Do you have to send a message of bad news or do you want to persuade? In this case, inductive sentence organization is best. Otherwise, deductive sentence organization is preferred. A few notes before you begin to write will be helpful here. (More exercises will be given to you in later chapters to help you develop your writing skills).

Writing

Once the planning stage is complete and you have organized your communication, write it. This will be a rough draft only. (This means that you will have to work on it a bit before the final version is ready to be sent.) Whether you write the rough draft using a computer or pencil and paper is unimportant. If you have word-processing skills, put them to use now.

You should leave your rough draft for 24 hours if you can. Sometimes new ideas come to you in the course of a day and you may see the subject in a different way.

Editing

Preferably 24 hours later, read over what you wrote the day before. Is the tone correct? Is your message clear for your reader? Will it achieve what you want it to achieve? Cross out any clumsy or unclear parts.

Make sure you have used precise, vivid words. If the message is one to convey bad news, general words will be more appropriate. Check your work in all areas. You will see that editing is a very important step. When you have done all you can, write the final draft.

Reviewing

The final step is to check the actual mechanics of the language of what you have written. Are all the words spelt correctly? Grammar correct? Punctuation perfect?

Hold the page out in front of you and look at the black writing on the white page. Is it neat and pleasing to the eye? Is it centred on the page? Are names, numbers and addresses correct?

In future chapters, you will be given practice in writing business communications. Use the P.O.W.E.R. formula for every piece of business writing that you do. So often, inexperienced writers begin writing business communications immediately, without giving a thought to the planning and the goal.

Exercise I

A   **Copy these groups of words. After each, write whether it is a sentence, a fragment, or a run-on sentence.**
1. Back in the days before computers.
2. Doing business must have been harder then.
3. People in business had to type everything.
4. Computer viruses spoil data they are difficult to kill.
5. Rarely spoke on the telephone.

B   **Add words to correct these sentence fragments. Write the new sentences.**
1. Travelled to Japan.
2. Many business executives.
3. The long, boring flight.

4. Called the customer.
5. Hundreds of products.
6. Japanese executives.
7. At 2 o'clock the secretaries.
8. Their desks.

C Correct these run-on sentences. Write the new sentences.

1. I telephoned the Sales Engineers they are flying with me to China.
2. Hong Kong is a fast-moving city the people here work hard.
3. He ordered 20,000 pieces we will ship them next week.
4. The Director chaired the meeting I took the minutes.
5. Mr. Yau telephoned this morning he seems to have a problem.

D Write ten sentences about a holiday that you have enjoyed or a country that you would like to visit. Check each one for fragments or run-on sentences.

E Rewrite the following sentence so that each thought follows on from the thought before. (You may have to change the words a little and vary the sentence lengths for the best results).

We are really very sorry that you found our products unsatisfactory. We will be shipping the new BCP pieces to you on the 17th. We hope that you will be happy with this arrangement. We will cover shipping costs of both these and the new products. Our sales engineers are confident that our new BCP components will be more compatible with your product.

F Copy these sentences. Add the correct word or words to complete each one.

1. A paragraph is _____.
2. The job of the detail sentences is to _____.
3. The single topic developed by a paragraph is its _____.

4. The last sentence of a paragraph may _____ or
_____ .

5. Writing the main idea as the first sentence and supporting or expanding it with detail sentences afterwards is called _____ .

G Rewrite the following sentences, changing the passive verbs into the active form:

1. The shipment was checked by the secretary.
2. The order was being processed by the clerk.
3. The products will be delivered by DHL.
4. The sales team has just been praised by the Sales Manager.
5. The shipment will have been checked by Mr.Wong.
6. The report had been written by the previous manager before he left.
7. The accounts are being looked at by the accountant now.
8. The file was lost by the personal assistant.

Exercise II

A Label the (a) phrases, (b) dependent clauses and (c) independent clauses in each sentence. Copy each sentence and attach labels.

1. We ate quickly at the restaurant.
2. She filed the papers in the boss's drawer.
3. The customer ordered 20,000 pieces in the afternoon.
4. This morning Mr. Lim received an urgent call.
5. Every so often the secretary has a holiday.
6. He told the manager about the deal.
7. Twenty minutes later, the plane took off.
8. He asked to see the boss, in his office, at 2 o'clock.
9. He couldn't get a flight out of China in time.
10. Don't call me, unless it's urgent.
11. Let me know if you can come.

12. I'll do it in the morning.

B   Write the following paragraph in sentences of suitable lengths to make it easier to understand.

There are over 70,000 merchant ships in the world some of these are general cargo ships others are specialized and are used for carrying one kind of cargo such as oil or bananas while others may be used for passengers or holiday cruises because people travel mostly by air nowadays the old passenger liners have gone out of service however it is still possible to travel by sea on a freighter (cargo boat) which has passenger accommodation.

C   Soften the following sentences containing bad news using the techniques you have learned.

1. I am sorry to tell you that I am rejecting your request for one month's leave.

2. Because of poor sales performance, sales staff will not receive the annual bonus this year.

D   Balance the following sentences.

1. The proofreading, editing, filing and storage of these documents is necessary.

2. Drinking, gambling, swearing and cigarettes are forbidden in the office.

3. Junior managers, middle managers, senior managers and all service engineers are invited to attend.

E   Change the following sentences from active into passive voice.

1. We can change the schedule.

2. They delivered the packages.

3. He posts the letters every morning.

4. She's typing it now.

5. They'll ship it on the 11th.

6. He was fixing it.

7. We had sent it before they called.
8. I could do it.
9. We should send it.
10. He would send it by Fedex.
11. I could have done it yesterday.
12. He should have sent it last week.
13. They would have delivered it last month.

F   Create unity between these pairs of sentences using repetition.

1. It is important that Mr. Wong receives the invoice for his order number XJJ6 no later than Tuesday next week. Please ask Ms. Lim to send it out before Friday.

2. Quality control is a very important part of manufacturing. It is therefore vital that all our sales executives are familiar with its entire process.

G   Create unity between these pairs of sentences using pronouns.

1. The customer ordered 200,000 pieces. 200,000 pieces is a significant order.

2. He flew to Sweden via the North Pole. Flying to Sweden via the North Pole enabled him to save some money.

3. The customer withdrew his order. The withdrawal of his order was unexpected.

4. The products showed signs of malfunction. The signs of malfunction were brought to the attention of the engineer.

5. The two sales managers flew to Singapore together. The two sales managers saw different customers, however.

H   Create unity between these pairs of sentences using transitional words and expressions.

1. The two managers flew to Singapore together. They saw different customers.

2. He performed very poorly. He was fired.

3. She achieved her quota. She was promoted.

4. Sometimes he performs well. Sometimes he performs badly.

5. He always spills his coffee on his papers. He always drops rice into his keyboard!

6. She's a great P.A.! She organizes my agenda so efficiently every day!

7. The customer has complained about the product. He has complained about the pricing too!

I   Here is a message written in sentences of all the same length. Rewrite it using sentences of different lengths.

Thank you for your order we received today. We will be shipping the products on 24th May. We confirm that you have ordered 120,000 pieces. Please note that the 25th and 26th of May are public holidays in the U.S. We will resume business on 27th May. Please confirm receipt of your order after then. Thank you.

Task I

Work in pairs. You want to write to your bank manager to ask him for a loan of HK$2,000,000 to put towards the purchase of a flat. With your partner, use P.O.W.E.R. to write this letter.

Task II

A   Say whether the following are paragraphs of deductive or inductive sentence organization. Give reasons!

1. Since the sixteenth century, when Peru was conquered by the armies of Spain, Spanish has been the only language used in government and business. In 1975, however, the Inca language "Quechua" was accepted on the same basis as Spanish.

Although Quechua is spoken mainly by the highland people, many Spanish-speaking Peruvians are also learning it. Today, both Spanish and Quechua are the official languages of Peru.

2. Chocolate is a food made from the seeds of a tree called the cacao. The cacao tree grows best in a warm, wet climate near the equator. Most of the world's cacao beans, or seeds, come from such an area in West Africa. Brazil also produces much of this raw material from which chocolate treats of all kinds are made.

B **Write a paragraph on any topic showing deductive sentence organization.**

C **Write a paragraph on any topic showing inductive sentence organization.**

4

Writing Memos

In this chapter, you will learn:
- direct and indirect writing methods;
- how to write informative, requesting and responsive memos using the direct writing method.

Memos (Memoranda) are simply communications among staff within a company. They are messages which are not addressed to outsiders. Memos may be sent from the CEO (Chief Executive Officer) to all staff, from a department head to all in his department, from a quality manager to department heads, or from the CEO to all division managers, for example.

As we saw in the last chapter, business communication can be deductive or inductive. Deductive sentence organization is also known as the direct writing method. Inductive sentence organization is also known as the indirect writing method. How do you know which writing method is best in what situation? The answer is that by thinking about what you want to say, and by imagining the response, you will be able to decide whether to use direct or indirect writing. This chapter will teach you to do that.

Most communications can be put into one of three categories:

1. ***Positive or neutral messages*** — the reader will either be pleased or will feel no emotion when he or she reads the message.

2. *Negative messages* — the reader will not be pleased when he or she reads the message.
3. *Persuasive messages* — the reader will not be interested in the message at first.

As we saw in the last chapter, inductive sentence organization (indirect writing) is more suitable for relaying bad news or for persuading. Deductive sentence organization (direct writing) is best for positive or neutral messages. In this chapter, you will learn how to use direct (deductive) writing techniques for memos.

You will use the direct method for learning how to write letters and replies to letters, and the indirect method for negative and persuasive communications.

Uses for Memos

Memos are an extremely important tool in business inside a company. They keep the business running, by letting different departments and departmental staff communicate with each other. Memos can be used to inform of changes, announce rules, explain processes, put telephone and meeting conversations into writing, record individuals' decisions and request information. They get information to many people without the need for meetings, and they make sure that all the people who need to know the message read the same message and can store it away for further reference.

If the message were spoken, this could not happen.

Memos save time and resources only if they are used intelligently and efficiently. However, some people waste time and resources by using memos inefficiently, for example, by writing a memo to one person when a phone call would be good enough, or by writing a memo for needless issues (e.g., toilet keys) or by sending the same memo to all staff even if most of the staff have no reason to read it.

To use memos efficiently, they should only be used for:

- putting important spoken information into writing,
- collecting information, and
- sending out important information when a meeting is impossible or unnecessary.

Most memos can be classed into one of four groups:

- informing
- requesting
- responding
- persuading

The first three groups use direct (deductive sentence organization) writing. Memos that inform, request and respond are what we will be looking at now.

The Well-Written Memo

Memos which are well written:

- begin with "To," "From," "Date," and "Subject" (Headings),
- discuss just one topic,
- are informal,
- are short.

Beside "to," is/are the name(s) of the reader(s). Beside "From," is the name of the sender. The date follows, and the subject, or topic, comes last. This is standardized form, which ensures that the memo can be filed away and found again easily.

A memo usually focuses on only one topic. This makes it easier to file. For example, if a memo covers two topics, it may be filed under the first topic, and the second topic would be forgotten. Because memos are only written to other members of staff within the company, they can be less formal than communications addressed to outsiders. It will be likely that you will know the reader, and so memos should sound as if you are having a conversation with him or her. The closer your relationship with the person who is to read your memo, the more informal the language of your memo can be.

You will remember the techniques you learned in previous chapters for writing concisely. These techniques also apply to memos. Memos should be short and to the point if you want your reader to appreciate them!

Types of Memos

Memos can be sent either on paper, or by e-mail over a computer network.

Standard (Paper) Memos

Some companies have their own specially printed memo-paper with "To, From, Date and Subject" already printed at the top. However, with computers and printers, it can sometimes be difficult to match up the text with these printed headings, and people using computers may just prefer to key in their own headings. Or a master copy can be saved on the computer, to be printed out when a memo is written.

When a memo is sent to more than one person, all names are listed, usually in alphabetical order, under the heading "To." Do not sign memos. It is usual to write your initials in ink after your printed name at "From." Senders of e-mail messages should key in their names at the end of the memo.

E-mail Messages

Many people in business nowadays send memos by e-mail. An e-mail message can be sent to someone sitting at the next desk, or to a colleague working in a subsidiary division half way around the world. E-mail works using computers, modems and software to send electronic communications over networks connected by telephone lines and satellites.

The message is kept in the "mailbox" of the receiver's computer until this mailbox is opened. An e-mail is in fact a paperless communication which can be treated just as if it were written on paper.

E-mail is useful in sending simple, relatively unimportant information. Longer, more complex or important messages are still better sent on paper.

To make most efficient use of the e-mail system:

1. Write your message first on a word processor and then upload it to the e-mail network.
2. Make your subject line attention-grabbing and precise.

3. Short lines and paragraphs are best. Lines under 60 letters in length suit small computer monitors. Eight lines should be the maximum for paragraphs. Leave a space between paragraphs for easier reading.

4. By using e-mail for sending informal messages, it is easy to become careless with grammar and spelling. However, like it or not, your writing says a lot about you to others. Some e-mail communications intended for one or two people only manage to get downloaded and distributed through the entire company to be read by everyone. If you know this may happen, you will understand that care is important.

5. Know that your message will not be private. Because of what may happen in (4), be extremely careful of what you write at all times. Just because the message disappears when you press "send" does not mean that it has been deleted. E-mail messages are permanent.

Direct Writing in Memos

The direct strategy (deductive sentence organization) is best for positive or neutral messages. You will remember that deductive sentence organization began with the main idea expressed in a topic sentence. Several detail sentences then follow, supporting and expanding this main idea.

The direct method gets to the point quickly, since the main idea comes first. Putting the main idea first has several benefits:

1. The reader wastes no time. He or she knows immediately what the message is about.

2. The reader quickly understands the rest of the message after reading the main idea, because they have been prepared for what is to come.

3. Putting the main idea first helps the writer better organize what he or she wants to say.

Don't forget that the direct method is best only if you know that the reader will not be displeased by your message. If you feel, for example, that the reader may disagree with what you propose in your memo, the indirect (inductive) method would be more appropriate, as you would be using persuasion to convince.

The first sentence of a memo should express the main idea

Your Memo-Writing Plan

So, you have already decided on whether you are going to use the direct or indirect writing method in your memo. As mentioned in the last chapter, you need a plan for all of your business writing. Later on in this book, you will learn several different plans for writing different messages. Writing a plan helps you to know what to say in your message and where to put what. At first, you will always have to write out a plan before you start. As you become more skilled, you will not need to rely on a written plan so much, until the time comes when you will not be using written plans at all. The plan will all be in your head.

Below is the plan for a memo that will please or be neutral to the reader:

🖎

TO:
FROM:
DATE:
SUBJECT: Briefly tells what the memo is about.

FIRST SENTENCE — gives the main idea.
BODY — (Main part, or message) — gives detail sentences to support/expand
the main idea.
CLOSE — states action to take, or summarizes the message.

You should have no trouble with writing who the message is to, who it is from, and the date. Your first piece of thinking will occur at "Subject."

This is the most important line of a memo, because it sums up the contents of the memo in just a few words. It should be short, yet still make sense. The subject line must also invite the busy executive to continue reading. If there is nothing to grab his attention, chances are he or she won't read it. So, a memo subject line should grab the attention, yet be short and to the point — a little like a newspaper headline. It should not be a full sentence and must not take more than one typed line. Here is an example of the "subject" for a memo that explains the procedure for the opening of a new office in China:

Subject: OPENING OF NEW CHINA OFFICE

The Main Idea

As we saw before in organizing paragraphs, the very first sentence — the topic sentence — expresses the main idea. Here is an example of an opening sentence for the above memo that explains the procedure for the opening of a new office in China:

Here is the schedule for the opening of our new office on Wednesday, 8th May in Xi'an.

Your opening sentence should *not* ask the reader to find information sent in an old memo. This is annoying and it is also rude. Instead, briefly review the important points of the other memo in this one, or attach a copy of the old memo.

Sometimes the first sentence will be the first paragraph although normally, a paragraph should consist of two or more sentences. If you need to say more to present the main idea, write a paragraph following the methods you have learned for unity and flow. However, as mentioned above, in most memos, the first paragraph is the topic sentence alone.

The Body of the Memo

The main idea is supported, explained and expanded in the body of the memo, through the detail sentences. In a memo, you will usually be either providing information or asking for information. In both cases, arrange the information in logical order. If you have to present a lot of data, take a separate paragraph for each topic. Use transitional words and expressions for smooth flow between paragraphs. Write clearly, using words you are certain your reader(s) will understand. Memos are written informally, so write them just as you would speak. Try not to use the words "I," "we," "mine" and "our" too much. Concentrate on constructing your sentences around the words "you" and "your" so that the reader feels that the message really is for him or her personally.

Memos which are short and to the point are best. It is good to present lists in memos, because items in a list are more readable and understandable than they would be if just written into a paragraph.

Compiling Lists

A list is a group of three or more related items. Information supplied in a list makes that information clearer, easier to read, and easier to understand. To write good lists, focus on two points: (1) the list itself, and (2) the sentence(s) that introduce the list.

The List Itself

Lists must balance. This means that you must write the items in the same grammatical format. For example:

Our goals for this month are the:
- Hiring of five sales staff
- Retrenching of two office workers
- Achieving of all sales quotas
- Reducing of costs

Here, "hiring of," "retrenching of," "achieving of," and "reducing of" all balance. The verbs are all presented in the same grammatical format. An example of a list which does not balance would be:

Our goals for this month are:
- Hiring 5 sales staff
- To retrench 2 office workers
- Achievement of all sales quotas
- Reducing costs.

Here, the items in the list are not balanced. Can you say why?

For memos giving instructions, put a verb first. This directs the reader's attention much better. For example:

To copy one A4 page using the new photocopier:
- Lift the lid
- Place the document face down within the A4 lines
- Close the lid
- Press the green button

Some lists are clearer with headings, as in the following example:

Here is the flight information for our visiting VIPs:

Name	Date	Flight	From	Arrival time
Tzing	18.2	BT123	Xi'an	18:32
Yamamoto	19.2	XL987	Tokyo	09:15
Wilson	19.2	CN765	Chicago	15:30
Dupont	20.2	PR654	Paris	10:00

Lists can be presented horizontally or vertically. Vertical lists stand out more and are much easier to read; however, they take up space. Horizontal lists show better that they are part of the sentence. They also take up less space.

Items in a horizontal list should be separated by commas, and the word "and" is placed between the last two items in the horizontal list. Here are two examples of horizontal lists:

Every morning, secretaries must check the schedules, collect and open all the incoming mail, respond to mail where appropriate, file documents, and photocopy important communications.

All sales executives must meet briefly in the conference room at 9 a.m. every Monday, Wednesday, Friday, and Saturday.

You will see that, for lists like these, it is not necessary to arrange the information vertically.

Introducing Your List with a Sentence

Try to give as much information as possible about the list in the sentence which introduces it. By doing this, you will avoid repeating words in the list itself. Compare the two lists below:

Poor introductory sentence and list	Good introductory sentence and list
All Sales Executives: • should try to achieve monthly quotas • should familiarize themselves more with their products • should try to achieve more personal relationships with customers	All Sales Executives should try to achieve: • monthly quotas • greater product knowledge • more personal customer relationships

Punctuation in Lists

Put a colon (:) after the sentence which introduces the list if your list is to be vertical. For example:

The following is the schedule for July:

Do not use a colon for a horizontal list. There is no need to punctuate the items in a vertical list. Good communicators use lists a lot in their memos because of their readability, and it will be very much worth your while to learn the above writing techniques for writing winning lists.

Ending Memos

Memos usually end in one of three ways:

- requesting action to be taken
- summarizing the information given in the memo
- closing with a thought

If you want your reader to take action, you need to state that very clearly, giving precise details.

Another way to end a memo is to make a summary of its important points. This is always appreciated by the reader if the memo is long and detailed.

If you do not want your reader to take some kind of action, and it is not necessary to summarize the memo (because it is simple enough to understand and/or is very short), then you may just end the memo with a final thought. As there is no need to write "Yours sincerely," "Best Wishes" etc. in a memo, the reader will find the memo with no final thought at the end somewhat abrupt. A memo should end with the following examples: "Let me know what you think," or, "I'd appreciate your feedback," or, "Is there any way we can fix this?"

Informative Memos

You may need to send out information in a memo, to be read by one person or more than one. Memos that give out information should be extremely clear and to the point. The direct method should be used. The following is an example of a memo which gives out information. It tells sales managers about a change in travel plans.

To: A. Chun, F. Fong, C. Wu
From: L. Siu, Sales Director
Date: 19th May 1998
Subject: CHANGE IN TRIP SCHEDULES

The following shows the new dates and itineraries for Sales Managers in June.

This change has taken place due to the arrival of the company President, Mr. Bill Glinton, from the U.S. at the end of May.

Date	Name	To	Customer
2.6	Chun	Japan	Mitsubisho
5.6	Fong	Singapore	Rotormola
6.6	Wu	Taiwan	Nikko
12.6	Chun	China	Nikei
18.6	Fong	Malaysia	Tomex
24.6	Chun	Malaysia	Tomex

Precise flight schedules will be available shortly.

Requesting Memos

Memos asking for information again take the direct method. (Remember, if you feel that the reader would be displeased by your request, the indirect method would be better).

You should always ask politely for information so that your reader will feel like supplying you with the information you want. If you do not ask politely, your reader will not want to respond!

Look at the following memo message asking for information:

I want you to find out exactly why this customer cancelled the order and I want you to do it immediately.

How would the reader feel on reading this? Remember, even if you are feeling angry, write your memos of request politely! How could you rewrite the above memo so that it sounds polite? For example:

Please could you find out exactly why the customer cancelled the order, before you do anything else? Thank you!

Here is a full example of a memo that asks for information. Requests should be written very clearly and be to the point.

To: P. Au
From: K. Chun, General Manager
Date: 18th January 1998
Subject: TOMEX SINGAPORE ORDER

Please could you give me the following information re. the order from Tomex Singapore?

1. Were the XT2 or the XT3 ordered?
2. How many pieces?
3. Terms of payment?

I need this information by tomorrow noon at the latest as I am speaking directly to the buyer tomorrow afternoon.

Remember to think over your message carefully before you begin to write. Your message may seem clear to you, but it may not be clear to the reader. Sometimes it is a good idea to ask a colleague to read your memo before you send it out.

Whenever possible in a memo asking for information, set a deadline for the reader at the end of your memo, along with a reason for this date/time (see an example of this in the memo above). This will allow the reader to organize his response to you in time. Mentioning a deadline and a reason is called end-dating.

For example:

Please let me have the president's schedule in Hong Kong no later than the 26th of May, as he will be arriving on 28th May and I need to finalize some points a couple of days before then.

Many memos requesting information are often written so that decisions, minor or important, can be made within the company.

Memos That Answer Other Memos or Documents

Someone may send you a memo or another document requesting information from you. You will have to write a memo which responds to that request. In this case, it is important to follow the three steps below:

1. Collect all the information you have been asked to provide.
2. Focus your thoughts.
3. Briefly outline the important points you want to send. If appropriate, you can use the document you received on which to make your outline, if you wish.

Again, begin the memo with a clear topic sentence (a sentence stating the main idea). A simple opening sentence could be: "Here is the information you requested about the sales meeting on the 28th."

Hopefully, the memo you received will have a clear list of what the writer wants from you! If this is the case, reply using a list yourself, matching his points with your own. Here is an example using the Tomex Singapore order request.

To: K. Chun
From: P. Au
Date: 19th January 1998
Subject: TOMEX SINGAPORE ORDER

Here is the information you requested on Tomex Singapore.

1. The XT3 components were ordered.
2. The order was for 200,000 pieces.
3. They are to be shipped out on 22nd January.

4. Payment terms are via telegraphic transfer, open account, net 30 days.

Hope this answers your questions. Let me know if you need any more information.

Finally, for typists of memos, use single spacing and leave one or one and a half inches for side margins. If you have no printed stationery on which to type a memo, you can do it on headed company stationery, or even on plain paper. Type in the headings. Begin typing on the 13th line for a full page, line 7 for half a page. The sender of the memo will initial it beside his or her typed name at "From."

This chapter has taught you to use the direct method when writing informal memos. In the next chapter, you will learn how to use the indirect method for formal letters that make requests.

Exercise I

A Answer the following questions.
1. Why are memos used within companies?
2. Explain the difference between direct and indirect writing strategies.
3. When are memos wasteful?
4. Explain the differences between internal communication within a company, and communication with outsiders.
5. What are the three types of memos, and what writing strategy is best for each?
6. What reader reaction would you expect for each of the three kinds of memos?
7. What are the four standard headings that appear at the top of memos, and in which order are they?
8. Why shouldn't a memo cover more than one topic?
9. Give the three ways to end a memo.
10. Why should a simple memo end with a final thought?
11. What are the four parts of the plan for memo writing?

12. Explain end-dating and why it is used.
13. What writing method do most memos use?

B Look at the following pairs of opening sentences. Say which one of each pair is an example of the direct method.

1. a. This will come into force at the beginning of March.
   b. For some time now we have been thinking of allowing our customers to pay using an open account, net 30 days.
2. a. From 12th February 1998, all packages between 10–25 kg are to be sent by Fedex.
   b. This will greatly speed up the delivery process.
3. a. The president's visit is now to include several countries in the region.
   b. We thought it would be a good idea to invite him to our factories in China and Thailand.
4. a. Sales representatives are invited to an intensive training seminar on the 10th of February in the Convention Centre.
   b. I believe that such an intensive training programme would be of great benefit to all sales representatives.

C Here are two memo opening paragraphs. They are too long and they are also indirect. Read through each carefully and identify the main idea. Then write an opening sentence that shows a more direct opening. Also give information for "To, From, Date and Subject."

1. A few of our sales executives have told me that they would be interested in going on an intensive sales training seminar as they believe it will increase their sales performance. I am giving persons who expressed an interest permission to attend this seminar — A. Chan, B. Fu, C. Kwok, D. Lam. The seminar is to be held on March the 18th.
2. I have managed to obtain big travel discounts for all Business Executives if we use Winsome Travel Company as our sole

agent. These discounts are available to you if you have a Winsome travel card. I am therefore arranging these travel cards for all Business Executives.

D

1. Rewrite the following paragraph in a horizontal list with an introductory sentence:

   The Regional Sales Manager will be attending our meetings in the mornings of Monday to Saturday inclusive next week, with the exception of Wednesday.

2. Use the following information to write a vertical list with an introductory sentence:

   In order to encourage feedback on company policy, we propose the placing of suggestion boxes in several locations around the company. Employees should feel free to drop a suggestion into any of the boxes at any time. A small reward will be given to employees whose suggestions are positive. However, employees can make anonymous suggestions if they wish. Suggestions are welcome from all members of staff, from the cleaners to senior management.

Exercise II

1. You are the head of a department. You notice that the memo-writing skills of your staff are substandard. You want to write a memo to the Training Manager requesting that he or she bring in a skilled business writer to run a two-day memo-writing course for your staff. You want the following topics covered in the course — the two kinds of writing methods, uses of memos, characteristics of memos, forms of memos, direct memos, the memo-writing plan, memos that request, memos that inform, and memos that respond. Write

the memo. Invent names and any other information that you think might be necessary.

2. The following request memo is badly written. Rewrite it giving corrections.

   To: G. Wong
   From: A. Tan
       I want to know the travel schedule for P. L. Lim for the month of February, I mean dates, countries and customers visited and the objectives of (reasons for) his visits.

3. Write a memo from the Training Manager to yourself that responds to (1) above.

4. The following badly written memo was written by G. Wong to A. Tan in response to (2) above. Rewrite the memo using what you have learned:

       P. L. Lim is going to Japan on the 3rd to sort out the problem with Tamagutchi, then he's off to Singapore to meet Rotormola that I think is a new buyer for him on the 9th, then to Taiwan to meet with Supercompany buyers on the 12th or maybe it's the 13th, I have to check, then finally to China to visit the manufacturing plant on the 16th.

5. You are the head of a department. Write a memo to everyone in your department announcing details of a new cost-reduction plan, which must reduce the operational costs by 25% across the company — travel, entertainment, telephone costs, communication costs, sundries, photocopies, etc. (Say in your memo that the information is on a separate attached sheet — there is no need to put it in the memo.) Invent any information that you think may be needed.

6. Here is a badly written memo meant to inform. Rewrite it correctly using the techniques that you have learned. Invent any data you feel is necessary.

To: Quality Assurance Department

From: K. Choi

This memo is for the Quality Assurance Department because I want to let you know that the order of 200,000 pieces of the XT3 components by Tomex in Singapore ordered on the 16th of February has been changed. Tomex Singapore now wants the XT2 components because they have found a fault in the XT3. It is up to you to correct the fault because when it is corrected they will place another order, this time for the XT3.

Task I

Work in pairs. Bring your revised memos into the class. Swop original (unmarked) memos with your partner. Revise your partner's originals (write on the original). When finished, compare your work. Discuss differences and agree on a common final correction.

Task II

Work in pairs. Collect three real-life memos each. To do this you will have to call or visit six companies (one memo from each company) explaining who you are and why you need one of their memos! (Practice for your communication skills!) Some companies will refuse — keep trying. However, most companies will not mind faxing or giving you one of their unimportant memos. Take three memos each, and photocopy each one.

On your own at home, revise each of your three memos for errors, based on what you have learned. (Write on the photocopy, not on the original).

5

Writing Letters of Persuasion/Sales

In this chapter, you will learn how to:
- use the indirect strategy for letters of persuasion;
- write effective claims letters;
- ask for favours effectively;
- express new ideas in memos that persuade;
- use the special techniques in sales letters;
- write effective sales letters.

If you agree that all businesses are based on selling in one form or another, you will understand that the skill of making others agree with and act upon your viewpoint is very important.

People who know how to convince other people are the ones who make decisions in business because it is their ideas which are acted upon. These people can become the most successful managers and business owners. The ability to influence other people is important in both business and personal success. Writing convincingly is only one area for success in business. This chapter will teach you to write successful letters of persuasion.

Requesting Persuasively

If you have to send a message where you want to change a person's mind, or where you want another person to take action, you must use persuasion. It is necessary to use persuasion when you think that the reader will not totally agree to your ideas, or when you need to organize your ideas well before you can express them.

Letters in which you must persuade are always more effective if they are written using the indirect method. The reasons and explanations for your ideas are much better accepted by the reader if they come before the main idea. If you feel that the reader will not agree with your ideas, you must set out your reasons clearly so that they seem justified to the reader. Perhaps more than any other kind of communication, a letter which persuades must follow a very well-thought-out plan.

The plan for letters which persuade is as follows:

1. *The beginning* — This captures the reader's attention and interests him or her in the next part of the letter.
2. *The persuasion* — This clearly explains the reason(s) for what you are asking, and their justification.
3. *The ending* — This politely and respectfully asks the reader to take action.

Asking for a Claim

Imagine that you have bought a new computer printer which keeps breaking down. You have had it serviced twice but it breaks down again. You decide to send a letter to the company to ask them to replace this printer. This would be a claim letter and you would have to use persuasion.

To write an effective claim letter, the first thing to think about is the ending!

You must have very clear in your mind what action you want the reader to take. In the printer example above, you want the company to replace your faulty printer. After you have decided what action you want the reader to take, you must then think of how you can justify your request, that is, how you can prove to the reader that what you are asking is reasonable and understandable. For example, if you want to make a claim to a business or a company on a faulty product, you can mention your previous confidence in the company's products and high business principles. It will be your reasons and explanations, after all, that will cause the reader to take the action you want.

Angry or rude letters will not get you the action you want. Claims letters are usually dealt with by the customer service department, and the reason for your claim will not be the fault of the person reading your letter! An angry letter may upset the reader, who will be in no mood to attend to your claim.

An effective claim letter arrests the attention of the reader in the opening, and leads the reader into the persuasion that will come. In the persuasion, you must give clear reasons to prove to the reader that your claim is reasonable and understandable. Using positive words, avoiding blame and staying calm are key factors in a successful claim request. Presenting your reasons and explanations in a logical order is also very important, and there should be a smooth transition through to the claim itself. In the ending, the action you want should also be very clear, and your request should always be polite and respectful.

The example of a claim letter below follows all the above points. The beginning captures the attention of the reader by saying something positive about the products. The reasons and explanations for the claim are written in logical order and shows that the claim is justified. Finally, the ending is polite and respectful, and states the action that the writer wants the reader to take.

✐

Dear Mr. Li,

For many years my family and I have been buying furniture exclusively from your store, FurnHome, and we have always been very pleased with the obvious quality of the furniture itself, and with the service we have been given, both in the store and during the delivery of our goods.

Last Wednesday I came to FurnHome to buy a dining table. I selected one, the "Regal 2000," and paid cash for it, and was told that the table would be delivered to my home on Friday morning. This was duly done, but when I unwrapped the table in my dining room, I discovered that one corner was quite seriously damaged.

I telephoned the store immediately, to be told by a Mrs. Fung in customer services that the store takes no responsibility for furniture after it has left the premises, and that nothing could be done. Mrs. Fung stated that, had I unwrapped the table in the presence of the delivery men, and brought the damage to their attention, FurnHome would in this case be able to take action.

I find this unacceptable. Obviously the table was damaged at some stage in the shipping and delivery process, as it was in perfect condition when I saw it, and I presume you did not intend to ship and deliver an already damaged table to me. I cannot believe that the policy of FurnHome is that "nothing can be done."

Please arrange for immediate replacement of this table. I hope that I will continue to enjoy the fine service I have been used to with FurnHome.

Yours sincerely

Asking for a Favour

When you ask someone for a favour, you are asking that person to do something for you with the understanding that he or she will get nothing in return. You may ask someone to do something for you that will take up their time, or use their money, or their knowledge. We all ask for favours from time to time, and they can be small favours, like asking somebody to pick up your mail from another location, or buying you a lunch box. When you ask for small favours, you can use the direct method, because you probably know the person well, and also because you do not think that the person will object too much to what you are asking. But some favours are big, and with big favours, you need to use the indirect method, and plan your approach very carefully. If you have to ask a very busy executive or well-known person to spend some of his or her time doing something for nothing — or very little — in return, skills of persuasion become very important. You expect that the reader will not want to do what you have to ask, and so the style of your writing must make him or her change his or her mind.

Look at the letter below. It is a badly written letter asking for a favour. You will notice that it uses the direct method by mentioning the main idea first, and so gives the reader a good reason to refuse. The body of the letter does not focus on the reader, but selfishly on the writer, and contains some negative statements. The ending does not clearly state the action that the reader wants, and is barely polite and respectful.

Dear Mr. Lo,

We would like you to come and speak to our writers' group this coming Friday the 13th of March at 7.30 p.m.

We know that you must be very busy, but we have all read your latest novel, *For the Love of the Tiger*, and we would be very pleased if you would come and discuss it with us. Your conception of the idea and writing techniques would be the most interesting for us, but as some of us are novice writers, please keep what you say very simple.

You would have to do this for free, but we would like to invite you to our monthly dinner on the 31st.

Yours sincerely

Rewrite this letter asking for the favour in the most effective way. The beginning should catch the reader's attention and interest, and persuade the reader that the writer values his talents and skills. Focus on the benefits the reader will enjoy by doing the favour and end with a clear request for the favour, politely and respectfully.

Here is an example:

Dear Mr. Lo,

Your latest novel, *For the Love of the Tiger*, was enjoyed tremendously by all the members of our local writers' group.

We have in fact formed a workshop and are currently working on suspense-writing techniques and plot development. As we all enjoyed your book so much, we have been working with it in our discussions.

For this reason we would be delighted if you could come and speak to us on Friday the 13th of March at 7.30 p.m., and spend an hour of your valuable time talking with us about the above strategies as you have used them in your novel. Although a fee to you would not be possible, we would be very pleased to have you as our guest of honour at our monthly dinner on the 31st of March.

Please call my mobile phone on 98765432 to confirm acceptance of our invitation to talk to us.

Yours sincerely

Writing Persuasive Memos

You will remember that memos are communications sent by employees to other employees within the same company. They are internal messages.

You may know very well the people to whom you send memos; they are your colleagues, and, as you know, memos are written informally. For these reasons you may feel that writing persuasive memos would take the direct method, where the main idea is stated first, followed by the explanations and reasons.

But consider writing a memo to your boss suggesting a new idea. Look at the memo below:

Hi Bill,

I think we should put the new sales plan to work as from tomorrow and not wait until next month as you suggested, because by waiting, we are wasting valuable potential revenue for the company.

Let me know what you think.

How do you think Bill, the boss, will feel when he reads this memo?

If you want to suggest new ideas at work, or ask your employees to take some new action, or ask them to accept new rules or regulations, you need to use the indirect method. This is because people do not like change, and they may not agree at first with what you are asking. You want them to read your reasons before they have a chance to object.

New ideas within an organization are usually not well accepted, and this is true if the ideas are directed upwards towards top management, or down towards subordinates, or across between colleagues of equal status. Change is not accepted for many reasons. Subordinates and colleagues may be lazy, and not want to change the track they are on. Upper management may resent the input of new ideas from below, and even may feel threatened by them. Sometimes an energetic, forward-thinking individual causes others to be jealous of him or her, and objection to the change the individual is proposing will be the result.

Whenever you want to propose new ideas that will result in change, you can expect objection. Knowing this in advance, you need to be ready with explanations and reasons which prove the worth of your ideas, and you also need to be able to make your reader(s) understand the benefits that this change will bring to them. Do not make the mistake of thinking that other people will immediately see how good your ideas are, just because you do. You need to be ready with solid reasons and explanations for your decisions.

Look at the memo below. It is an example of an effective memo of persuasion. You will see that it catches the reader's attention by mentioning something that the writer knows will be interesting to the reader. It explains the reason before suggesting the new idea and answers objections before the reader has a chance to question the writer's ideas. It gives the advantages that the reader will enjoy and ends with the request for action which is respectful and polite.

To: Bill, Manager for Administration
From: James, Marketing Manager
Date: 8th October 1998
Subject: MS. LAM

I was very pleased to see that you have recruited so quickly Ms. Lam, a new receptionist, to take the place of Ms. Yee on sick leave.

Although she has been with us for only two weeks, there can be no doubt that Ms. Lam is a very competent receptionist in many areas, and having a competent person as the first point of telephone contact for customers is very important for a company. Politeness is also essential, but I have, however, been receiving complaints from customers about her abrupt manner on the telephone and would be pleased, therefore, if you could have a word with her about this. Obviously you were not to know her telephone manner from interviewing her, but business will be much better for all of us if she would be polite to customers on the telephone.

Please would you speak to Ms. Lam within 12 hours and get back to me with feedback on her response? Thanks.

Letters Requesting Purchase

How do you write a communication which asks people to buy your products, your ideas, your goods or services, or even yourself? Such letters are called sales letters. Sales letters are very special requests, especially since all business is based on selling — in fact every letter is a sales letter to some degree. We try to sell our ideas, our image, ourselves. Sales letters use very special techniques and strategies. Learning these techniques and strategies to use in your own sales letters will be of great value to you.

Very often in business you will have to persuade or to promote. Often also, you will be the receiver of sales letters — other people will try to persuade you to buy. Very often, people will buy if the sales letter was effectively written. If you learn how an effective sales letter is written, it will help you to decide whether you want to buy something because you really need it, or just because the sales communication persuaded you to.

Again, sales letters have a plan:

1. The beginning — Once again the beginning catches the attention of the reader.
2. The body — This part focuses on the needs of the reader, and the reason why the reader would want the product (the selling point). In the body, the price of the product is quietly mentioned.
3. The ending — The ending of a sales letter encourages the reader to buy the product.

What Is to Be Sold? Who Is the Reader?

Before an effective sales letter can be written, the writer needs to think very carefully about the product to be sold, and about his market, that is, the person or people whom the writer wants to buy his or her product. You, the writer, must know everything there is to know about the product which is to be sold. Not only must you need to know everything about your product, you must also learn as much as possible about the products of your competitors, so that you can focus on the strengths of your product compared to the weaknesses of the products of the competition.

The best sales letters are sent to an especially chosen market. For example, the manufacturer of a sewing machine would target mailing lists of people who read sewing magazines. The writer of the sales letters to this selective market would have very clear ideas about the kind of person who reads the magazines — sex, age range, occupation, income, hobbies, etc. This would enable the writer to tailor-make his sales letter to have the greatest and widest appeal to the people in his market. If the writer of sales letters does not have a small select market, he or she is forced to write his or her sales letters to a more generalized market, which he or she will not have specific information about.

Grabbing the Attention of the Reader

Sales letters which have not been asked for (unsolicited sales letters) are generally not well received. In fact, they are sometimes called "junk mail," because they are unwanted, and go straight into the rubbish bin. For this reason it is extremely important to grab the reader's attention so that he or she will, hopefully, keep on reading. The specialists in direct mail marketing have researched very thoroughly the strategies which work best in attention-grabbing statements. These can come in many forms, for example:

1. An offer. ("A free encyclopaedia is waiting for you when you send your reply to us!")

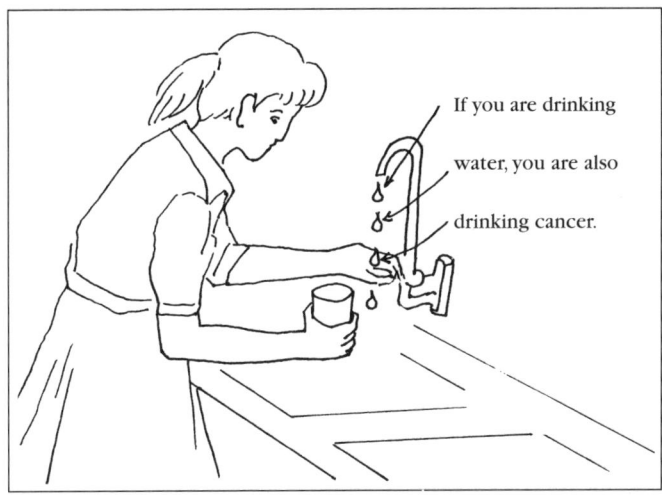

You can get the reader's attention by using shocking statements

2. A feature. ("Subscribing to our magazine will make you eligible for our offer of a timeshare property!")

3. An address-opening. ("We are sure, Mrs. Wong, that you would like to earn some extra cash!")

4. A shocking statement. ("If you are drinking tap water, you are also drinking cancer.")

5. A story. ("Usually to the effect of: Mrs. X did this, Mrs. Y bought our product and did that. Look at Mrs. Y now! Poor Mrs. X! She should have bought our product too, to enjoy what Mrs. Y has got!")

6. A bargain. ("Two air tickets for the price of one can be yours!")

7. A solution to a problem. ("Still fat? Tried everything? Try Wait-Off!")

8. A proverb. ("Every journey begins with the first step. Your first step is to fly with us, for the journey of a lifetime.")

9. A question. ("Do you really enjoy cooking for three hours every night?")

Making the Reader Want to Buy the Product

How do writers of sales letters persuade the readers of their letters to want to buy or try the product? There are two ways: by stirring up the emotions of the reader, or by stirring up his or her rational thought.

Writers who influence the emotions write to stir anger, sadness, fear, love and happiness. Writing to stimulate the five senses — seeing, touching, tasting, smelling and hearing — are also effective ways of influencing the emotions. The writer of successful sales letters will try to influence the emotions if the product is cheap, cannot last for a long time, or is not an important item to have. Writers promoting holiday packages, for example, will try to appeal to the emotions of the reader.

Writers of sales letters about money, saving money, investing, insurance and financial planning try to influence the reader's rational thought. The writer of successful sales letters will try to influence the reader's rational thought if the product is expensive, can last for a long time, or is an item valuable for future investment in either health or financial security.

Banks and other financial institutions and companies, for example, will try to appeal to the rational thinking of the reader.

However, many very successful writers of sales letters try to appeal to both the emotions and the rationale, with the focus on rational thought, the emotional appeal having a lesser focus.

Focus on Why the Customer Needs the Product

A product may have many selling points, that is, reasons why the customer would need it. However, your sales letter must have focus. It is commonly thought that by mentioning all the wonderful features of a product, the customer will be even more willing to buy. Nothing could be further from the truth.

Focus on only one or two of the product's selling points, because by pointing out everything, the reader will be confused. Before you begin your letter, you should analyse the reader's precise needs, and so in your sales letter you can match the needs of the reader to one or two of the product's selling points, thus creating the best possible chances for the reader to want the product.

Building Customer Want

In your sales letters, you will have to write in such a way that the reader wants to have the product. There are several ways to do this:

1. By focusing on the benefits the reader will enjoy by buying the product, e.g., "By using our highly concentrated dish washing liquid, you will save money, as cost per use is very little."

2. By using vivid adjectives and detail to describe the product, e.g., "Here you are looking at an emerald-green Mercedes with the softest cream leather seats and polished cherrywood surround."

3. By using "cool" language. Avoid words like "fantastic," "tremendous," "wonderful," "sensational," "awesome," etc. They sound false and can cause readers to resist your message.

4. By showing confidence in your product. Mention a 30/60/90-day, money-back guarantee, a warranty, a free sample. If a well-known company or person uses your product, mention it.

5. By using what other people say about the product. Include testimonials from other buyers and users of your product. For example, "This dish washing liquid is wonderful! Just one litre lasted my family of five months!"

How, When and Where to Mention the Price

If the price of your product is very affordable, or is discounted to a great degree, mention this at the beginning of your sales letter. If the price would be somewhat prohibitive, do not mention it until after you have created the want in the reader for the product. Some sales letters do not mention the price at all, but include the price in an enclosed order form. Other ways to break the news of the price are to:

1. Present the price in small amounts. For example, if the price of a weight-loss product is $1,000 per month for the customer, you could present this information by saying that the cost is only $33.30 per day.
2. Make it clear to the reader how he or she will be saving money. For example, by using a very concentrated cleaner, money will be saved long-term.
3. State how much better value your product is compared with similar products manufactured by the competition. For example, the values of an Electroluxy vacuum cleaner over the competitors are stronger suction and better cleaning effect.
4. Offer your product at a bargain price. For example, an introductory offer, or a discount if the customer buys immediately, or buys a certain quantity of the product.
5. Combine the price of the product with the advantages the reader will enjoy. For instance, "for as little as $33 per day, you can achieve the slim figure you have always wanted."

Getting the Reader to Buy

The ending of a sales letter is crucial. It must "close the sale," that is, ask the reader to buy. There are several ways to do this:

1. Give clear instructions. Tell the reader exactly what to do, e.g.:

- "Complete the enclosed form."
- "Call this number now!"
2. Ensure that it is very easy for the reader to order and pay, e.g.:
   - "Just call our 24-hour operators and quote your credit card number."
   - "Order now, pay later!"
   - "Order today and enjoy our credit terms!"
3. Offer a bargain, e.g.:
   - "10% discount if you buy before the 19th!"
   - "We will include the extra product X if you buy now!"
4. State a deadline, e.g.:
   - "This offer only lasts until the end of March!"

Below is an example of a successful sales letter. It advertises a doll, "Sweetheart," using a sales letter to people on a mailing list. A full coloured picture of the doll accompanies the sales letter.

✍

Dear Valued Customer,

If there is a little girl in your life, she will love our doll!

Wearing a floral lavender and rose dress, "Sweetheart" is dressed perfectly for a day of love from the little girl in your life. Her coordinating shirt is accented with eyelet lace, and an embroidered collar with a beautiful flower. She even has a matching sun-hat.

Sweetheart's precious, sweet smile and bright green eyes are sure to capture your little girl's heart the moment she sees her. She's only four convenient instalments of $222, and that's only a total of $888 which includes postage and handling!

And we promise you a 100% money-back guarantee for one full year!

Please respond before 21st February 1998. Simply fill out the form and send to the address below. SEND NO MONEY NOW! You will be billed for the first instalment before we ship you your doll. Please respond promptly: dolls are produced in a limited edition.

So enjoy the special innocence of little "Sweetheart" by placing your order today!

A doll is not an important item to have in life. Therefore, the writer of this sales letter tries to stir up the emotions of the reader, by asking the reader to think of a little girl in his or her life, and by saying how much the reader's little girl would love this doll. The words "Sweetheart" and "love" also play on the reader's emotions — these words bring the feelings the reader has for a little girl up to the surface.

The doll's clothes are described using vivid adjectives so that the reader can almost see the real doll and touch it, thus building up want in the reader. Imagining the little girl seeing the doll for the first time also does this very effectively.

The price is mentioned in small affordable units, which further bring the reader to the point of buying. The total price is $888, which in Hong Kong is a highly acceptable figure! This is another strategy making the reader decide to buy. The actual process of buying is very simple as the writer asks the reader just to fill in an order form and send it to the address. There is no need to send money, and the writer builds trust in the reader for the product by mentioning the money-back guarantee.

The reader is further encouraged to act quickly by the fact that there is a deadline for orders. Finally, the reader is told that this doll is produced in a limited edition. This means that only a small number of them are manufactured, and this can further push the reader to buy. The last sentence sums up the whole aim of this sales letter — buy the doll!

Being able to write persuasively is a very valuable asset to anyone in business. As mentioned at the beginning of this chapter, all business operates on the idea of being able to sell something to someone, whether a product, an idea or even oneself! But the ability to persuade goes beyond writing business letters and memos persuasively. If you can organize your reasons and explanations into logical sequence, you can much more clearly present your case and defend your views orally, in life in general.

Exercise I

As a class, discuss the following questions:

A

1. Why is it important in business to be able to influence people?
2. People do not like change. True or false?
3. Why in general do people not like change in the workplace?
4. Why is it important to understand and recognize the skills used in sales letters?
5. Are sales letters like favour request letters or are they different?

B

1. What is all business based on?
2. What makes a good manager/leader?
3. Why are letters of persuasion more effective when written using the indirect method?
4. What is a claim? Give an example.
5. List two things you would mention in a claim letter.
6. What reaction would you expect to a letter of persuasion?
7. Why is it not a good idea to be rude and show anger in letters of persuasion?
8. List some of the ways in which claim letters, favour request letters and persuasive request memos are all similar.
9. Why is it best if you can target a sales letter to a small select audience?
10. What are the disadvantages of sales letters which target large numbers of the general population?
11. List the most important parts of a sales letter.
12. When do writers of sales letters appeal to the emotions? To the rationale?

Exercise II

State three mistakes in each of the following four letters of persuasion using what you have learned. Then rewrite the letters to make effective letters of persuasion.

A

Dear Mr. Fong,

I want a cash refund. Last week I bought a very expensive leather jacket from your shop, it cost me all of my month's salary. When I got it home and put it on, the zipper stuck on the lining. As I was trying to free the lining from the zipper, it tore.

I think it is a disgrace that such an expensive jacket should have such a problem. I took the jacket back to the shop but the man who sold the jacket to me said that I would have to put my complaint in writing to you.

Also he would not consider my complaint as I have lost the receipt of the jacket, although of course he must remember me.

If this is the way your shop does business, I am not impressed. If you do not give me a cash refund for this jacket, I will be seeking legal action through my solicitor, and you can guarantee that neither I nor my friends will go near your shop again.

Yours angrily

B

Dear Ms. Lee,

We are a group of four teachers very involved with counselling students on personal issues. Unfortunately none of us is trained in counselling and we were wondering if you would be willing to run a short counselling training course for us over, say four to six weeks.

We have approached the school where we work which has in turn spoken to the Department of Education, but they are not willing to fund you. So you would have to do it for free, I'm afraid, but we are sure that we would benefit greatly from what you would have to teach us and for that reason it would be well worth your time to do it. You would also have to provide the premises, as the school is unwilling to host someone not solicited by the Department of Education.

You can start on the first Monday in March and every following Monday after that. 7–9 p.m. is the time that suits us best.

Yours sincerely

C

To: ALL STAFF

From: Gary Ling, Head of Resources

Date: 22nd February 1998

Subject: WASTING RESOURCES

I am sick and tired of seeing fax and copier paper being wasted so much in my department. I am aware of needless telephone calls and memos which are going out, and I know that several members of staff are using our lines to make personal phone calls. I also know about un-updated mailing lists and the paper wastage that results from letters going to people who will never read them.

Please change these bad habits immediately. Do you think that the Earth has an unlimited supply of resources? Do you imagine that resources for this company are free? Or shall I propose that all wastage be taken out of your salaries in future?

Please clean up your act now.

D

Dear Reader,

If you don't buy our air purifier immediately, you must be crazy. Our is the best on the market, it is a well-known fact.

Hong Kong's air is very polluted. Whenever you go outside, pollutants in the air get into your lungs and they can seriously damage your health. So why should you continue abusing your lungs at work?

Modern Hong Kong offices have windows which cannot be opened, and offices are air-conditioned all year long. Just because the air is cold does not mean it is fresh! In fact, with every breath you are inhaling air which is constantly being recycled — old air. If the air-conditioners in your office are not 100% clean, they will also be blowing spores and bacteria into the air you breathe. Do you wonder why you get sick so much? As if that wasn't enough, if you work with smokers, the quality of the air you all share will be very greatly reduced.

Our air-purifier will rid your office of dust, bacteria, spores and smoke. It will also generate negative ions, which are good for your health and well-being. We are selling this top-of-the-range machine for only $2,999; delivery anywhere in Hong Kong is $300 extra. A fully detailed instruction manual comes with the machine.

So buy now, and save your lungs from doom!

Task I

Work with a partner. Acquire three sales letters and photocopy each. One of you work with the three photocopies, the other with the three originals. At home, answer the following questions about each sales letter. (Do not contact your partner to discuss!)

1. What is the product?
2. Is the product expensive or inexpensive, long-lasting or short-lasting, necessary or unnecessary to have?
3. What market does the letter target? (i.e., who are the readers?)
4. Can you identify a beginning, a body and an ending?
5. Does it capture the reader's attention?
6. Using what strategy?
7. Does it target the emotions or the rationale? Why?
8. Does it highlight one or two selling points?
9. How does it make the reader want the product?
10. How is the price introduced?

11. List all the ways that the ordering/paying process is made easy.
12. Does the closing of the letter prompt the reader to buy?
13. Would you buy the product? Why/why not?
14. What other comments and/or observations do you have about any or all of these sales letters?
15. Do you think they were well-thought-out and well-written?

Task II

With your partner, bring your three sales letters and the questions and your answers into class. Compare your answers to the questions you answered at home, and discuss with your partner.

6

Letters and Memos That Carry Negative News

In this chapter, you will learn:
- why you need to use indirect writing when you send bad news;
- to use the six parts of an indirect message;
- to refuse requests skilfully;
- to remain polite when you write refusals.

You will remember that whenever you communicate, you should first think about the reaction that it will have on the person who is going to read it. If you think that the message is going to upset or to annoy the reader, it is better to use the indirect method of writing rather than the direct method. You may remember that in the indirect method, reasons and explanations are given before the main idea. If someone has bad news for you, usually they will try to make the news easier for you to take by giving you reasons first, and then tell you the bad news at the end. This is the indirect method.

In business, many communications give bad news. In fact, bad news is very common. You may have to refuse quotes, reject job applicants, delay shipping or delivery, refuse credit, tell of redundancies, cutbacks and downsizing, say no to invitations and many other things.

In this chapter you will learn how to use the indirect method to give bad news.

If somebody has good news to tell you, you will want to hear it quickly. Usually somebody who gives you good news, tells you before giving you the reasons for the good news. You may not even be interested in the reasons! Good news, therefore, is told using the direct method.

The direct method is not good for bad news. Going straight into the bad news first can easily upset or anger the reader. He or she will then certainly not be in the mood to listen to reasons, or to try to understand them. Worst of all, the reader may not want to even read the rest of the message. For these reasons, the whole idea of the indirect method for sending bad news is for letting the reader read the reasons before reading the disappointing message.

There are, however, some cases in which the direct method is better for giving bad news, for example, if you know the reader very well, or if you know that the reader is a person who appreciates directness. Or you may prefer to use the direct method of giving bad news if you have tried the indirect method and it has not worked, that is, if your reader is a person who does not easily take "no" for an answer. But in general, bad news is always better received by the reader if you use the indirect method.

When we send a message telling bad news, there is a special six-point format which tells bad news most effectively. As mentioned before, explanations and reasons are given first in an indirect message, with the bad news coming at the end. Below are the six points which are used to deliver the most effective bad-news messages:

- The buffer
- The transition
- The explanation
- The bad news
- The alternatives
- The friendly closing

Using the Indirect Method

Before you use the indirect method, you have to think of the reasons for the bad news that you are going to give. Your reasons and explanations come first, remember, and if you do not have any good reasons for sending the negative message, you will not be able to write effectively. Therefore, the entire letter depends upon its reasons and explanations for it to be convincing.

The Buffer

However, all messages which are going to give bad news must begin with a buffer. A buffer is a tool which lessens shock. Writing a buffer will put the reader into a mood that will make him want to continue reading your message. As we saw before, we want the reader to read the whole message, and writing something that will put him in a good mood will help to do just that.

A buffer should be three things:

1. It should be neutral. This means that the buffer does not hint at the bad news which is to come. It also means that the buffer does not make the reader think that there will be good news in the message.
2. It should say something positive for the reader.
3. It should be relevant; that is, it should mention the situation in question. A buffer which talks about the local football team's winning victory may be neutral and positive, but it is not relevant to business.

Some examples of buffer sentences are as follows:

1. A buffer in a bad-news letter telling a job applicant that he or she was not hired:

I was very pleased to talk to you last week about what you do and the first-class training programme in Wisconsin.

2. A buffer in a bad-news letter telling a customer that he cannot have a refund:

Purchasing our "President" ostrich-skin briefcase was a wise decision, Mr. Chiu, as these rare cases represent the highest quality of workmanship in the world.

3.   A buffer in a bad-news letter refusing an invitation:

I am very impressed with the effort you have put into making the upcoming Achievers Banquet an occasion not to be missed.

The Transition

After the opening buffer statement, the reader needs to be transited to the explanation that is going to follow. This transition can be done most effectively using a selection of the transitional words or phrases you have already learned. Avoid the transitional words "but," "however," or "unfortunately," because they give the reader an idea of the bad news that is to come. Skilful writers will use key ideas or words from the buffer or the transition sentences that will naturally lead to the bad news that follows.

Read the following sentences. They are transitions which go with the buffers shown in examples 1–3 above:

1.   Buffer:

I was very pleased to talk to you last week about what you do and the first-class training programme in Wisconsin.

Transition:

Your sales knowhow will no doubt have benefited greatly from this training which in turn will add value to your experience.

2.   Buffer:

Purchasing our "President" ostrich-skin briefcase was a wise decision, Mr. Chiu, as these rare cases represent the highest quality of workmanship in the world.

Transition:

As you know, this is a limited edition; each item is carefully handcrafted in our German factories, and is given a serial number and a signed guarantee of its authenticity.

3. Buffer:

    I am very impressed with the effort you have put into making the upcoming Achievers Banquet an occasion not to be missed.

    Transition:

    I have always been delighted to attend this annual function and I am sure it will again be a great success.

The Explanation

A successful negative letter will have a well-presented explanation. The reasons for the bad news are the most important part of the negative letter. Without good reasons for the bad news, the letter will not be effective, even if it is written very well. The explanation is the main reason for using the indirect method. We want our reader to understand our explanation before breaking the bad news.

Again, as with the transition, avoid using the transitional words "but," "however," or "unfortunately," because they warn the reader of the bad news to come. You should show in your explanation that you have thought very carefully about the situation, and write very clearly your reasons for refusal or rejection.

In your explanation, simply present the facts. Be unemotional and objective, and give the impression that you want to help. If you have more than one reason for refusing, denying or rejecting, give the strongest reason in your explanation. Then give the bad news. After that, support the bad news with the other, weaker reasons for refusing.

The Bad News

In Chapter 3, we looked at ways to make a negative message softer.

Now we will look at these ways in more detail and use them as you learn to write messages giving bad news. Here are some effective techniques:

1. Do not put the bad news where the reader will see it immediately — this means not putting it in the first or last sentence of the letter, and also not putting it in the first or last sentence of any of the paragraphs in the body of the letter! Bad news should be put in the middle of a sentence or paragraph halfway through your letter.

2. Put the bad news in a long sentence — short sentences get straight to the point and can be blunt. Putting bad news in a long sentence helps to soften it, and also in the same sentence you can make an offer of help or suggest an alternative.

3. Put the bad news with a dependent clause — you may remember from an earlier chapter the difference between a dependent and an independent clause. To refresh your memory, look at the following example.

Although it's after office hours, we can process your order.

In the above sentence, the clause "we can process your order" is independent because it makes sense when it stands alone. The other clause in the sentence, "Although it's after office hours," is a dependent clause (also known as a subordinate clause) because it depends on the independent clause to survive. It cannot stand on its own and make sense.

You should put bad news with a dependent clause. This makes the reader think about it less. Usually, it is the independent clause which the reader notices most. Which clause did you feel was stronger in the example above? "Although it's after office hours," or, "we can process your order"?

Here are two examples of bad news hidden in dependent clauses.

Although payment cannot be made by cheque, we will accept visacard with pleasure.

As the item you want is no longer in stock, please accept a voucher with our compliments.

Dependent clauses typically begin with "as," "although," "since" or "because."

Note that in these two examples, the tone of the independent clause is also positive, and is placed last in the sentence. These two techniques are also very effective in giving bad news.

4. Use passive verb forms — you have learned in Chapter 3 that using the passive voice softens bad news. "We cannot grant your request" (active voice) is more upsetting than "your request cannot be granted" (passive voice). The passive voice emphasizes actions, not people, and it helps you to be objective and neutral.

5. Express yourself clearly but without unnecessary detail — bad news should be clear but it is unnecessary to give every single little detail. The following bad news is unnecessarily strong:

I have to inform you, all junior staff, that as from this evening we will have to make you redundant. It is illegal to leave your place of work without signing a dismissal form; failure to do so will result in police investigation.

Here is the same message, written clearly, but without the over-strong detail:

As all junior staff will be made redundant after today, in keeping with legal requirements, please sign a dismissal form this evening.

6. Hint at a refusal — sometimes, you do not have to be direct about refusing someone or something. For example, instead of saying "I cannot come to your company's annual dinner," you can write "Although on that evening I have another engagement, I would be delighted to attend on a future occasion."

Here, the refusal is very indirect, because you have merely implied that you cannot attend this time. But if you use this technique, be very sure that the reader will understand your message, especially if the message is for someone whose first language is not English. A message which says, "Thank you very much for your invitation. I would be delighted to attend on a future occasion," may be misunderstood by a non-native English speaker, who may well think that you want to attend this time and next time! You don't want to have to write another message explaining your first one.

The Alternatives

After giving the bad news, offer help. This is known as the alternatives. For example, you could suggest another action to take, or you might offer the reader a compromise or a substitute, or direct the person to an organization which may be able to offer more help. Here are two examples.

✍️

Although I will be unable to give the presentation in Tokyo, my capable colleague, Billy Wong, will be standing in for me.

Our company does not supply the information you are looking for; however the Chamber of Commerce may be able to help you.

However, in some negative messages, there may be no alternatives you can offer. If this is the case, there is nothing you can do; just move on to the closing, which, in a letter with no alternatives, should be particularly friendly and positive.

The Friendly Closing

After preparing the reader for bad news through effective reasons and explanations, and then giving this bad news, with alternatives, you come to the end of your negative message. The closing should be friendly. This is to tell your reader that you still want good feelings to exist between you and him or her. The ending should be positive, if possible, with a sentence or two which will make the reader feel better after the bad news.

In a letter where you reject a job applicant, you can close with:

Close a letter that carries negative news with goodwill

✍

We will be keeping your application on file and we will contact you if a suitable opening arises.

At the end of bad-news messages to customers, close your letter so that the customer knows that you want to continue doing business with him or her:

✍

I am enclosing a waiver for the shipping payment of 15% of your next order, and we look forward to serving you soon.

There are four points to remember in your closing lines. These are:

1. Do not mention the bad news again in closing. Close with friendly, positive comments. You do not have to drag the bad news up again.
2. Do not apologize. You have clearly stated your reasons for the bad news and you feel strongly that these reasons are justified. You have no need to say you are sorry in the closing.

3. Do not use clichés in the closing. Clichés, as you learned in an earlier chapter, are expressions which are so old and used that they are now meaningless. Your reader will feel that you are being insincere and will not want to believe your message. For example, "I look forward to hearing from you sooner or later."

4. Do not ask your reader to contact you regarding the bad news. "Please do not hesitate to contact me if you have any questions about this matter" is unnecessary. You are telling the reader that the issue is still open to discussion. You have clearly stated your reasons for the bad news, and your decision is final.

Refusing Requests

In business, you will be asked to do things which you cannot do or do not want to do. In such a case, you must refuse. Again, your first step is to imagine the reaction of the person who requested something of you. If you think that the person will be upset, or hurt, or annoyed, or even angry by your refusal, you should use the indirect approach, following the six-point plan discussed above, i.e.:

1. *Buffer* — opens with a neutral, positive, relevant comment.
2. *Transition* — uses key words or ideas to lead naturally to the explanation.
3. *Explanation* — gives clear reasons for the refusal, without the use of certain transitional words which give a clue to the bad news.
4. *Bad News* — uses a long sentence in the passive voice in a dependent clause, in the middle of the message; can be hinted at instead of directly stated.
5. *Alternatives* — suggests ways to help (if an alternative exists).
6. *Closing* — brings back good feelings; is positive and does not mention the refusal; does not contain clichés and does not apologize.

Look at the following letter of refusal.

Dear Mr. Nakajimo,

   I am sorry but we cannot possibly get your components shipped out to you by the date that you would like. This is because there is a production problem at the factory in China which will not be solved before the shipment date you require. Trying to force the problem to be solved just because you want your products shipped by that date will only lead to unrest among production workers, which could well be the trigger for civil unrest in Shenzhen, given the present dissatisfaction among factory workers as they strike for higher wages.

Again, I am sorry about not getting your products to you on time; please do not hesitate to contact me at your earliest convenience to discuss the matter.

Most sincerely yours

Does this letter of refusal begin with a buffer? Is there a natural transition from the buffer to the explanation using a key idea or words? Does the explanation give clear reasons which do not go into detail? Is the bad news softened with a long sentence, the passive voice, in a dependent clause? Is an alternative offered? What is wrong with the closing? Has this letter been written using the indirect method?

(You will rewrite this letter in the exercises at the end of the chapter.)

Refusing Claims

All businesses run on the concept of selling to customers, in one form or another. Sometimes, customers may ask for a price reduction on products, or may ask to have more products for the same price if the order is a big one.

They may ask for favours in other ways, for example free delivery or at least a minimal delivery charge. Sometimes, even employees may ask for big discounts on the company's products, or other favours. These favours are called claims.

Often, a company will approve reasonable claims to show the customer or employee what a good and generous company it is, because of course they want to encourage the customer to continue buying their products. But some claims cannot be approved because the claim is unreasonable, or because the claimant is misinformed, or even dishonest.

In such cases a letter refusing the claim must be sent out. Because the refusal is bad news, the indirect method is used. The writer gives explanations and reasons for refusing the claim first, then delivers the bad news later. This gives the writer a chance to explain his or her reasons before the reader realizes the message is negative.

Imagine a situation in which a customer has written to company A saying that the product he bought from company A is being sold more cheaply by another company, company B. He is asking for the price difference to be refunded to him by company A. This claim is refused, because in fact the two products are not exactly the same. Here is the letter of refusal:

Dear Mr. Wu,

Your decision to purchase the air purifier from us was a wise one, Mr. Wu. You can be assured that we are always proud to sell the highest-quality products at lowest prices. (1)

We are so confident in our business policy that we do indeed offer the price-match refund to our customers if they can prove a cheaper price to us offered by another retail store. Proof can be in the form of an advertisement, which you have, correctly, enclosed. (2)

Our product retails at $1,999. The product in the advertisement you sent retails at $1,399, a difference of $600. This advertisement describes an older model of the air purifier. Your purifier combines the very latest hi-tech features, which are missing from the earlier version. (3)

You have bought the best air purifier on the market today, Mr. Wu. Should you wish to install it in your car, the enclosed manual will be of help. We place great value on your custom and we look forward to serving you again soon. (4)

Notice in this letter that the buffer (1) is neutral, relevant and positive. The transition (2) prepares the reader for the explanation that follows. The transition mentions the idea of other-company advertisements telling of more cheaply advertised products. The advertisement is also mentioned in the explanation (3). You will see that the bad news is actually implied in this letter — it is cleverly built into the explanation. The writer does not actually openly state that the customer cannot have the difference on the price. The ending (4) renews good feelings in the reader. He is praised for his good shopping sense and enjoys a sense of value as a consumer. Furthermore, a free manual is an offer of help.

Refusing Credit

Simply put, credit means acquiring products, goods, services, or a loan of money before paying for them, and paying later with interest.

Banks and other major institutions refuse claims for credit very frequently, and for this they commonly use a standard letter which they send to everyone, regardless of the individual case involved. This kind of letter is called a form letter, and they are convenient for the institution to send out, simply because a bank or institution has to deal with so many cases.

If you have ever received a form letter refusing you credit, you will understand the feelings of the reader. Even if you know that you are a poor credit risk, you feel annoyed that you have been treated to an impersonal rejection. Form letters sent out by major institutions are not only often inappropriate to the reader's individual case, but stop the reader from wanting to do business in future with that company. Just because a person or a company is a poor credit risk now does not mean to say that the same person or company will also be a poor credit risk in the future.

It is, therefore, to your advantage to write a personalized letter for each credit refusal you send. This helps to keep business relations favourable. Again, you follow the indirect method for credit refusals. The news is bad, and you must allow yourself to explain why the credit must be refused before the reader realizes the bad news and starts to object.

Again, the six-point plan is used: Buffer, Transition, Explanation, Bad News, Alternatives, and Closing

Here is a letter refusing credit:

✍

Dear Mr. Wu,

We are delighted to be able to supply you with our XYZ components, more so since they have shown a 100% compatibility with your JJ Steam Iron. (1)

Because of the particular suitability of our components to your product, we are keen to begin shipment immediately. (2)

Although on review of AABB's credit report, credit terms cannot be offered to you at this time, we would be more than delighted to work with you on a credit basis when the financial standing of your company improves. A copy of the AABB report is enclosed. (3)

In the meantime, a cash arrangement can most easily be established. By buying only 1,000 pieces today, you will receive a 5% cash discount. On the sale of your irons installed with our components, order another 1,000 pieces, again paying cash. By doing this, you will be using the most suitable components on the market for your irons, enjoying a cash discount with no loss to your inventory. (4)

We are proud of the exceptional quality of our components and look forward to servicing your own products both now and in the future. (5)

You can see that the buffer in this letter is neutral, positive and relevant (1). The transition (2) continues the idea of product compatibility, and leads the customer to understand that the writer is keen to see his products being sold. This puts the reader in a very receptive frame of mind. The bad news is told at (3). You will notice that the news is put in a dependent clause, using the passive voice, and that the sentence containing it is long. The independent clause ("we would be more than delighted ... improves") is very positive, giving the reader hope for the future. The alternative (4) is both possible for the customer, and positive. The good-will ending (5) renews good feelings in the reader and brings him to understand, again, that the writer cares about his products.

As you may realize, the subject of credit is a very delicate issue. A person or a company is exposing their complete financial situation to you. If the finances of the person or the company were healthy, they would not be asking you for credit, and so a request for credit will usually be from a person or a company whose financial standing is questionable.

You may want the business of this customer, but only if you know that he or she can pay when payment is due. If the applicant's credit history is good, you will be more likely to grant credit. If the applicant's credit history is poor, you will (you should!) refuse credit. If you have to refuse credit to a customer, it will therefore be because you know that he or she will very unlikely be able to pay when payment is due. Refusing a customer credit is in fact telling him or her that you know he or she cannot afford the payments. This can be embarrassing to the customer, so it is extremely important that your credit refusal is one which not only "saves the customer's face," but also which ensures continued business with that customer in the future.

There are three main goals to aim for when writing a credit refusal, given that refusing credit is such a delicate issue. These are:

1. Avoid using language that upsets or hurts the reader, so making him or her not want to do business with you in future.
2. Keep the customer but on a cash basis.
3. Prepare the customer for the possibility of credit in the future without giving false ideas.

    If doing business with American companies, or for businesses within the United States, there would be a fourth goal:
4. Avoid giving too many details for the reason for the credit refusal, which could lead to an attempt by the customer to sue.

Customers who ask you for credit and are refused will usually keep doing business with you. It is therefore very important that you encourage their business by sensitive, understanding, and respectful credit refusal letters.

The credit refusal letter in the example above is one which is sure to keep the business of the customer, Mr. Wu. You will see that it encompasses all the above points.

The Indirect Strategy — Is It Honest?

You may feel that the indirect strategy is not completely honest. Delayed bad news? Long, dependent clauses? Passive voice? Negative message hidden in the text? How can this be honest?

But turn it around, and look what would happen if you used the direct method for bad news, as in the example below:

Dear Mr. Wong,

I am sorry but we cannot give you credit you asked us for because our credit-reporting agency has told us that you have a very bad credit record.

Does this sound good? This kind of communication is direct and straight to the point, but it hurts the feelings of the reader. Hurting people is unnecessary.

There is a way to give bad news gently, and the indirect method is the way to go. The police and the medical profession have to break bad news very often. They do it orally, by talking, but they too, usually use the indirect method. People can handle bad news much better if it has been told to them in the correct way. Sometimes, people are more upset by the way the bad news was given to them than the bad news itself!

Any business communication is perfectly ethical if it does not intend to deceive. By using the indirect method, your motive is not to deceive the reader or hide the news, it just gives you a way to present the news in the kindest possible way for the reader. The indirect method does not hide the truth or change it.

The Indirect Strategy in Other Situations

You have learned that the indirect method is best for delivering bad news. This is true for most written communications and in this chapter, you have learned how to apply the indirect method to letters giving bad news. But the indirect method can be used in other situations also.

As mentioned above, policemen and doctors often have to tell people bad news, and they do this by telling the listener face-to-face. You too can use the indirect method to tell people bad news in a face-to-face situations. If you have damaged your friend's car, if you have changed your mind about marrying your girl/boyfriend, if you cannot repay a loan to a friend, you can use the indirect method to give the bad news orally, and so adapting it to all kinds of different situations in your life.

You might find it interesting to listen to bearers of bad news, for example in television dramas, and judge whether they use the indirect or direct method! Did they give the bad news well? How could they have said it better?

REMEMBER! Do not use "although" and "but" in the same sentence!

Exercise I

A   Answer the following questions.

1. What kind of reader reaction would you expect for you to use the indirect method?
2. Give the six-point plan for giving bad news, in the correct order.
3. Describe a buffer. Where do you place it in the message?
4. Give three features of an effective buffer.
5. Describe an effective transition between the beginning of the message and the explanation.
6. Give seven ways to make a bad news message most effective.
7. Give four things that you should not write in the closing.
8. Give three transitional words which you should never use in bad-news messages.
9. Tell the four positions in a letter which stand out more than the others.
10. Give the best position in a message for the bad news.
11. Give two reasons why the direct method is not the best for bad-news messages.
12. When is a message dishonest?

B   Put the following bad news into dependent clauses beginning with "as," "although," "since" or "because." Write the whole sentence for each.

1. We no longer manufacture the component Sg876. We manufacture another component, the Sg877. We would like to send you a sample of this.

2. We cannot refund your money without a receipt from you. But we would be happy to give you a credit voucher.
3. The company will not pay for non-company entertainment expenses of managers. The company will pay for the running of company cars.

C   Change the following bad news into the passive voice.
1. I cannot give you permission to smoke in this office.
2. We cannot give you credit on this occasion.
3. We do not allow personal telephone calls to be made from this office.
4. We are delaying your shipment until next month.
5. I cannot grant this claim for you at this time.

D   Say which sentences are good buffers.
1. I was delighted to meet with you at the trade fair in Chicago last week.
2. Isn't the weather terrible at the moment!
3. I'm sure you were as pleased as I was about our football team's victory at the weekend.
4. You made a wise decision in purchasing our product, Mr. Lee.

E   Change this letter of refusal to write a skilful one, using the six-point plan. Invent any necessary information.
Dear Mr. Nakajimo,

I am sorry but we cannot possibly get your components shipped out to you by the date that you would like. This is because there is a production problem at the factory in China which will not be solved before the shipment date you require. Trying to force the problem to be solved just because you want your products shipped by that date will only lead to unrest among production workers, which could well be the trigger for civil unrest in Shenzhen, given the present dissatisfaction among factory workers as they strike for higher wages.

Again, I am sorry about not getting your products to you on time; please do not hesitate to contact me at your earliest convenience to discuss the matter.

Most sincerely yours

Exercise II

A   Correct the following bad request refusal.

Dear Mr. Lee,

Thank you for inviting me to be the MC at your company's annual awards dinner on January the 15th.

I am very sorry but I have another more important appointment on that night.

Hoping you can find somebody else, wishing you all the best.

Yours sincerely

B   Correct the following bad credit refusal.

Dear Ms. Wong,

Thank you for submitting a credit application to us for the products you want to buy. However, we have checked your company's credit record using AABB Credit Information Services and have just read their report. I am afraid to say that we cannot give you credit on your products because your company's credit record is very poor. So we will be treating you as a cash-only customer.

We are looking forward to receiving your first order and payment by cash.

Yours sincerely

C   Correct the following bad claim refusal.

Dear Mr. Tamagotchu,

I have just received your order for 5,000 of our GHJ components, and I note that you want a 15% cash discount on them.

However, as you are well aware, our discount for cash payments is 10% and not 15%, so I am afraid that a 15% discount will not be possible for you. Furthermore, you are a new customer, and I would only be prepared to consider giving a higher discount to a well-established customer. This means that you will have to buy from us for two years at least.

Sorry about this, but I am sure that any other company selling these products would say the same. We are processing your order immediately.

Yours sincerely

Task I

Obtain three bad-news letters from companies. List some of the major faults in these messages.

Task II

Bring your three corrected bad-news photocopies into the class. Swop originals with your partner and correct them in class. Compare your corrections with your partner's and agree on a final correction. Rewrite your three correctly.

7

Trade Negotiations

In this chapter, you will learn:
- what negotiation is;
- the nine communication skills used in successful negotiations;
- the key success factors of a good negotiator.

What Is Negotiation?

"Negotiation" is simply a process in which we communicate, with one or more persons, in order to arrive at what we want in certain confrontational or conflictual situations.

When we hear the word "negotiations," we usually imagine high-powered executives cutting million-dollar deals with multi-billion dollar companies in New York, Tokyo, or London; or between the representative of one country negotiating with the representative of another country for the release of a political prisoner. These scenarios could be true, and do happen.

However, negotiations in everyday life can also be as simple as a conversation between two or more people or organizations discussing what it is that they want out of a situation. Literally anything can be negotiated, from a six-year-old child bargaining for another helping of ice-cream from his parents, to employer and employee negotiating the terms of an employment contract; or from the CEO (Chief Executive

Officer) of a multi-national corporation negotiating a take-over bid, to the police negotiating with kidnappers over the release of hostages. Because anything can be negotiated, it is outside the scope of this chapter, and indeed of this book, to present every possible negotiating scenario. What we are going to cover instead are the very basic ground rules and skills for any negotiation situation, which can be applied, therefore, to any situation involving negotiation, business or otherwise. Obviously, in this chapter, we will be looking at negotiation in business.

We Are All Negotiators

Just as each one of us is in some form a salesperson, we are also negotiators, perhaps without realizing it, from early childhood right up until the present day. In daily life, we generally negotiate to ensure that we get what we want, or achieve the best result out of a situation. These negotiations are often carried out with our colleagues, employers, friends, relatives, families, shopkeepers etc. If we think about our daily activities, they often consist of many negotiation examples such as asking for a lower price of an item we wish to purchase, asking our parents if we can stay out a little longer, staying up for another hour before going to bed or demanding a certain report be completed by certain date so that we can get on with our portion of the work etc.

Negotiation Is Integral to Trade and Business

Negotiations happen and are needed in business and trade. Countries realize that they must trade their goods and services in order to stay in the world's economic system, and if they want to increase their wealth. Some countries trade to get the goods and services they need, and other countries trade to sell products and services to foreign, thus enlarged, markets for a return in funds. People, countries, and nations trade, unfortunately, for reasons of self-interest — out of necessity or to earn a profit — rather than for humanitarian goodwill. Because of this self-interest, many trade situations are somewhat conflictual or confrontational because each side's own interests are at stake. This inherent tension creates an attitude of "What I want is more important than any good I would do you." This is the heart of trading, and trade takes place by making offers and counter-offers. In other words, bargaining, or negotiating.

Negotiation Is a Vital and Necessary Process

As we have said earlier on, negotiation is a communication process which usually implies that solutions and settlements are reached through a succession of verbal give and take. However, it is unlikely that you would want to accept immediately the first offer from the other side, unless, of course, the offer is exactly what you want!

Successful Negotiation Is Searching for Compromise

In negotiation, there are at times situations where only one side can be considered as having won. In fact, children negotiating with parents probably give the best examples of this. A discontented child may hold his breath until he is blue in the face while negotiating for his wants, and a parent will usually give in to him after such a hard tactic, thus ending up the loser. However, as we will see later on, this is not the best negotiation outcome for a business situation.

In business, one is often involved in negotiations with other parties and companies in order to get what one wants. Ideally, we would want all parties to be involved in the negotiation to be happy and satisfied with the outcome of the discussion, and this should be the objective of all the negotiators as far as possible. This is so because we want most business relationships to be long-term, and it does not make any sense in a negotiation to "win" everything, so that the other party is left with feelings of defeat and humiliation. If this were the case, it is unlikely that the business relationship could continue with mutual benefit for too long. And if the relationship were to terminate, both parties would end up being the losers.

Negotiating for a Win-Win Outcome

An issue which is to be negotiated may be a very simple one, but the negotiation process may become very intense if the issue is important to both sides, in which consequences would extend far into the future.

Negotiations in business, as mentioned above, result in both sides being happy with the outcome, or at least, happy because each side feels that the other has not got the better deal — that the outcome was fair.

As we said, negotiation is not about beating the other side. Instead negotiation is a vital and necessary process through which we all achieve, to one degree or another, what we wish to accomplish of out of any situation. In this sense, negotiations serve a very important purpose in business, trade, political or day-to-day activities. By negotiating, you aim to strike a deal with the other side where both of you are happy with the arrangement. The "I win-you win" outcome is the goal of any skilful negotiator.

Negotiation Can Be Learned

Like other communication skills, negotiation skills, fortunately, can be learned. At the most simple level, there are nine basic negotiation skills to be mastered. Here they are:

Being Able to State What the Negotiation Is Trying to Achieve

To state what you want, use the present tense, and use assertive language, e.g.:

What I want from this meeting is an agreement on the amount of rental to be paid by my office.

Obviously the people who are negotiating must keep in mind what it is they want out of the negotiation. This can include an idea of what they are prepared to "give" the other side. An experienced negotiator will also have the skill of being able to bring the discussion back on track if it appears to be going away from the objectives.

When stating objectives at the beginning of a negotiating session, you simply tell the other side what it is that you want out of the situation.

Skilful negotiators use assertive language. Below-average negotiators use weak language to express what they want. Assertive language is much more likely to capture the attention of the other party, and is also a statement to the other side that you are serious. Here is the difference:

Assertive language	Weak language
I (don't) want	I would(n't) like
I (don't) need	I would rather (not)
I must	I feel
I insist	I hope
I require	I wish
And in conversational form, some examples:	
What I/we (don't) want is	What I/we would(n't) like is
What I/we (don't) need is	I/we would rather (not) have
I/we must have	I/we feel we should have
What I/we insist on is	I/we hope that
What I/we require is	What I/we would like to see is

Tell the other party what it is that you want, and tell them what you would be willing to trade, to get it.

Being Able to Set Your Objectives within a Range

What I want from this meeting is an agreement on the amount of rental to be paid by my office.

Experienced negotiators set objectives within a range, rather than within an immovable point. Look at the example above. The negotiator here is experienced. In his head, his objective lies within a range. In his head, he thinks, "I will accept any rent increase from zero to ten percent." He does not say:

What I want from this meeting is for you to agree to a five percent increase in
office rental, no more.

He keeps his objective within a range, and expresses it that way to
state his objective. He knows that the actual amount can be negotiated in
the discussion. In another example below, a skilful negotiator sets her
objective within a range:

What I want from this meeting is an agreement on the price of your products.

In her head, she knows the exact figures in her range, although she
does not express them at the beginning of the negotiation.

Being Able to Summarize What the Negotiation Is Trying to Achieve

So, we agree that we are meeting to come to a decision on the proposed
increase in office rents.

State in clear and simple language what it is that both sides are
trying to achieve. The words "so, we agree that we are meeting to ..." is
a good way to start a summary of negotiation objectives.

The objectives of the meeting must be very clear in the mind of the
negotiator if he or she is to be able to summarize it. The other side in the
negotiation may have different objectives from you. It helps, obviously,
if both parties have the same objective (for example, an initial agreement to begin a shipping process), but in many cases of negotiation, the
objectives will be different. When these differences have been resolved,
the common objective should be summarized so that both sides are
absolutely clear about what the negotiation is about. Summarizing is
very important for negotiating, because negotiations can become very
heated and emotional. The subject under negotiation can be lost under a
mass of pointless comments which lead far away from the objectives.
Even more confusing, areas which have already been covered can be
covered and covered again. A summary in the middle of all these

refocuses all concerned, can calm the atmosphere if tempers are beginning to show, is often regarded as refreshing by negotiators. To bring the issue back into focus, you can say:

I would just like to give a reminder that we are meeting today to ...

You will see that it is important to summarize:

1. what has been said about the issues under negotiation,
2. the proposals from each side,
3. what the differences are on each side,
4. what has been agreed.

Summaries should be very brief. They should also be objective, fair and equally cover both parties. A summary which is unbalanced and favours one side can create hostility.

It is important to summarize at all stages of the negotiation, not just the objectives. Always summarize if anger is beginning to appear in the negotiation, summarize immediately after your proposal(s), summarize when you are asking if both parties agree, and finally, summarize when agreement has been reached, to clarify it for both sides and also to assure yourself that what you think has been agreed is actually what the other side has also agreed.

Being Able to Create a Plan for the Negotiation

Keep it very simple. Understand that it may fall apart in the negotiation, because the other side may come up with something unexpected. Try to anticipate what the other side's plan will be. Have a back-up plan ready for yourself.

Negotiation is a step-by-step process, with each step coming from the alternate sides. As you sit down to negotiate, neither side will know the outcome. But having a plan to follow will help.

Following some sort of set plan helps greatly in negotiating. Obviously you can only plan for your side, and not for the other party. Your plan should aim to meet the objectives that you have set; your objectives should be set within a negotiable range. Your plan should be kept simple, and it should also be flexible. A rigid plan will not work in the negotiating arena. If the first step in your plan is to get the other side to, for example, explain how an office owner arrives at such a high rental increase, you may start by saying:

✎

Perhaps we could start by listening to your viewpoints why such a steep increase is warranted.

Another example of starting off a plan:

✎

Let's start by looking at your previous payment record, and then talk about your new credit request. Does this make sense?

Here is a simple plan drawn up by the representative of a company who is about to enter into a negotiation with the office landlord. The building owner is proposing a 20% rental increase on all office units, which the company is not prepared to pay.

Before the negotiation, the company representative does his "homework." He tries to do as much of the following as possible:

1. Find out the market rental for the area the office is located and for other parts of the city in general.
2. Find out the general rate of rental increase for the area for commercial buildings.
3. Find out if there are many vacancies around the area and in the city in general.
4. Know the present rate of inflation.
5. Be aware of any changes that are planned for the area which could affect the attractiveness of the area positively or negatively.
6. Find out as much as you can about the negotiating party — his personality, negotiating style etc.

From his investigation, the representative comes to realize the following:

1. Current rental before the increase is in line with the market.
2. The general rate of increase is below that of inflation because the economy is depressed, and there are many office vacancies in the area and in the city in general.
3. The present rate of inflation is around 9%.
4. The government has already approved a plan to build an overpass over the nearby roundabout to ease traffic, and this should be seen as positive for the area. Furthermore, a car park for the area is being proposed and is under the government's scrutiny presently. Once accepted, this will ease parking problems greatly.

Consequent to what he has found out, the company representative makes the following plan for his negotiation:

1. The company wants to stay put if at all possible, that is, they do not wish to move if they have the choice. Therefore, it is in its interest to reach an agreement with the landlord.
2. The maximum increase (the exit point) it will accept is 12%, it being significantly more than the current average rate of increase of between 7–9%, but it does mean that it does not need to move, and all the interruption and costs that go with the removal.
3. It will enter into the negotiation by asking the landlord to justify the reason for such a large increase, and then it will present all the hard data why it thinks the landlord should reduce rental instead of raising it!
4. It hopes to reach a settlement at around inflation rate, i.e., 9%.
5. If all fails and no agreement can be reached at this desired level, it will then revert to accept the maximum of 12% as a preference to a breakdown in negotiation, because the company's negotiating objective is to stay where it is if the cost of staying can be negotiated to a reasonable amount.

With this plan prepared, the company representative has something that will guide him through the negotiation. He knows what tactics to employ, and precisely at what point he should just walk out, even though he may not want to! We will see later on in our example of an negotiation how this plan can help him achieve his objective.

To be thoroughly prepared to achieve his objective, the representative should also have a back-up plan. A back-up plan is only reverted to when the negotiation is not going well or is not going according to the original plan. This is clearly the second best plan.

For example, his back-up plan for the above scenario might be that if the landlord still does not budge even at 12%, then he might consider using one of the following as a second best way forward. What he will end up using will depend on many factors. The possible back-up moves may be to:

1. threaten to link up with other office tenants to boycott such an unreasonable increase, or
2. threaten to take the case to some judiciary or arbitration body because it is felt that the increase is not reasonable and is way above the current market rate of increase.

The above are confrontational and may not be the best choices available or appropriate. Milder and perhaps more effective ways might be to:

1. offer to take up tenancy for a longer term (e.g., for a 3-year tenancy instead of a 2-year one) at the exit position of the negotiation plan, i.e., at 12%, or
2. agree to the asked for rate of increase of 20% but ask for it to be delayed by one year or some other time frame, and try to negotiate the first year to the target rate of 9%, or, failing that, to the exit rate of 12%.

Being Able to Put Forward Offers and Counter-offers

Make conditional offers. Use the first conditional tense.

✍

If you do this, we might be able to do that.

This is the essence of negotiating. Putting your offers across, handling the offers of the other side and putting up counter-offers are what

Always use conditional statements in negotiations

negotiating is all about. Being able to make your offer clearly is a skill that can be learned.

You negotiate offers (proposals), nothing else. In fact, a proposal can be seen as a suggested outcome to the entire negotiation. During negotiations, it is important to be able to make proposals skilfully if you want to get what you want out of the negotiation.

To be most effective, a proposal should be very clear about what you want the other side to do, without saying too much about what you would offer in return, because you want to put forward a proposition and keep your offer from the other side at the same time. State proposals briefly and do not give long explanations for your proposals. Summarize them immediately after you have made them.

Offers are made using the conditional tense in English. "If you give me this, I will give you that." Use the conditional tense to state your conditions which you would like to settle the issue. State what you want, be vague about what you could trade, e.g.:

- " We could possibly do this, if you will do that."

- " If you do this, we could consider that."
- " This could be possible, if you would agree to that."

The whole tone of the negotiations will depend on how you put your proposals forward, and therefore how they will be received by the other party. Listen to the answers from the other side, and consider each issue objectively. Summarize what they have said, to check your understanding.

Being Able to Handle Unacceptable Proposals Put Forward by the Other Side

The other party will put forward offers which are not acceptable to you. Your verbal reactions to these must be skilful and clear.

You must also then come up with counter-offers, which tell the other side that you are not happy with the offer they have proposed and offer new suggestions from your side. Both the handling of the other side's offers, and the counter-offers you make must be put forward very carefully if the mood of the negotiation is to be kept favourable.

If you do not agree to the terms of a proposal put forward by the other side, you put forward a counter-proposal. A skilful negotiator knows how to handle proposals which the other party puts forward, to his or her own advantage. It is important to reject the other side's propositions delicately, so as not to cause talks to break down. On the other hand, it is never good to accept any proposition from the other side immediately. When the other side makes a proposal, try to understand the thinking behind the proposal. For examples:

✍

While we understand the rationality behind your proposal, we just find it too restrictive and limited, would you reconsider the following aspects again ...

Your proposal is straightforward and does cover many of our concerns, however, we just find the timing for its implementation slightly long, would you be able to bring this forward a little?

I realize it is not easy for your company to meet all our requests, however, cost and lead time are two areas that we cannot compromise on. As for the other points, we can give a little and accept most of what you offered. Would you mind reassessing your proposal and let me have a definite reply by tomorrow morning at the latest?

Being Able to Recap and Clarify What Has Been Said

Experienced negotiators return repeatedly to what has been said and summarize the important and relevant points. This helps to keep the information crystal clear in the minds of both parties. In the negotiation process, you can ask if you can summarize:

Can I just summarize the main points of what we've covered before we continue, so that we're all agreed on what has been decided?

Being Able to Summarize Agreements

Agreement between negotiators must be carefully summarized. This keeps the negotiation on track and shows that objectives are being reached for:

So we're all agreed on X.

We've agreed that we can do this, if you can do that.

For a negative statement:

It appears that we have not come to an agreement about X.

Being Able to Promise Future Action If No Outcome Is Reached on This Occasion

Sometimes, negotiation breaks down. This is because neither side is willing to accept or even consider the offers and counter-offers of the other, at some stage in the negotiation. As long as you are sure that agreement can be possible in the future, you should agree to resume discussions at a later date. At best, this gives both parties time to rethink the negotiation, which may well lead to a change in objective on one or both sides.

Also, the person doing the negotiating may not have the power to make the final decisions, but must instead report back to a relevant authority. Again, this gives that party more time in which to make a decision:

I/we'll get back to you as soon as I/we have the boss's decision.

I/we'll let you know as soon as I/we hear from Japan.

That's a good point. I don't have the authority to answer you on that one; I'll get back to you just as soon as I have the answer.

I need to put it to my wife. When I have her feedback, I'll let you know.

In all negotiations, remain polite and try to remain objective with the person you are negotiating with. Listening is extremely important. Try to listen more than you talk, because only by listening will you learn what is in the heads of the other side. Listening is especially important after you put forward a proposal, after you summarize anything, after you ask a question, and after you reach an agreement. In each of the above situations, you must wait until the other side answers before you talk again. Learn to feel comfortable with silences, even long silences.

To recap, top negotiators:

- put their objectives into a range rather than into a fixed point;
- do not make instant counter-proposals;
- use the indirect method for disagreeing — give their reasons first, then disagree;
- summarize frequently to test their own understanding of how the negotiation is proceeding;
- ask a great number of questions;
- recap many times on what has been said during the negotiation;
- listen more than they talk;
- aim for an "I win-you win" outcome.

Here is an imaginary negotiation scenario between the landlord of a certain office space in Times Square and the representative of a company, who rents an office from this owner. The owner wishes to increase the rental by 20%. The company is not prepared to pay such a large increase. Before he negotiates, the company representative draws up his negotiation and his back-up plan as presented earlier on.

This example gives several of the nine negotiation skills outlined above, but because it is rather short, it cannot give all. Which of the nine points are given in the following example?

Rep.: *Good morning. Thank you for coming. I will go straight to the point. Our company was shocked when we received your notice expressing your wish to increase the rental by as much as 20%, effective from the next tenancy term onwards. The purpose of our meeting today is to arrive at a more reasonable rate of increase for the rental. Let us begin by saying that the proposed rate of 20% is way too much, as we understand the market rate of increase in the city is less than 10%! We are interested in understanding how your company arrives at such a dramatic increase!*

Landlord: *Your company has been a good tenant to us, and we thank you for the past business. However, as you know, the cost of living has been edging up surely and progressively more each year, as well as the fact that the current interest rate for mortgage repayments is very high. Furthermore, we have only made a token adjustment in the rent during the last tenancy renewal as you can probably recall.*

Rep.: *That is true and we appreciated it a lot, and hence we continue to choose to stay where we are, whereas we could have chosen to move on had it been otherwise. This is how we feel right now with this rate of augmentation; we would be paying above market rental. This would be hard to justify to our headquarters while the economy had been hit so badly recently and business is going through some tough and critical cycles. With this rental, one obvious option we have is not to extend the tenancy, which will not be good for us nor for you, as I presume you would want some continuity in this, especially from such a reputable company as ours which has always paid rent on time and has always been a good corporate tenant in every other aspect. My objective of calling this meeting today is to explore with you in an open-minded fashion any other alternatives that might be acceptable to both of us. My objective this morning is therefore an agreement with you on the next term of tenancy which is due to start in a few months' time. Do you think this makes sense?*

Landlord: *Yes, I definitely can't argue with the kind of records your company has shown us — you have been a dream tenant that any landlord would love to have. I realize that the rate of increase we ask for may be viewed as high, but I trust you do see the value of staying in such a convenient location in town, and with this the savings in costs and time that your employees enjoy because of the office's proximity to major transportation hubs and commercial centres and facilities. Sometimes, these benefits can't be simply quantified, but they are there and are very real.*

Rep.:   *Sometimes its convenience is exactly its drawback. Because it is so central, it is often congested with heavy traffic at rush hours, and the parking during any time of the day is a real challenge and a real test for anyone's patience! However, I do agree that problems such as these could be overcome if one were to take the MTR instead. Still, when we realize that we could have the same size of office for about 15–20% cheaper in a neighbouring town, we can't help but consider why we are spending such hard-earned money on unnecessarily high rents! You see my point of view?*

Landlord: *Yes and no. As regards to the traffic and parking problems, you may know that the government is in the thick of planning to build a flyover nearby here; when this happens, the traffic should ease up significantly. Also, the government is building a 13-storey high parking lot right beside us! When this is ready, this will become the hottest property in town!*

Rep.: *All probably true, but we are talking about events that are 2–4 years down the road, they really do not have immediate impact on our business right now. There is no way that I can accept this increase of 20%. In actual fact, we were tempted to seek your permission to reduce rental this year because of the bad economy and the fact that many offices are now vacant, and there are clearly very good bargains around. We are prepared to move if that's what it takes to contain our costs!*

Landlord: *Since you feel so strongly about this issue, how do you see we could resolve this issue?*

Rep.: *Well, given the current circumstances, I would find it hard to accept more than what the market rate of increase is right now, which I believe is around 7%! This is very much less from what you have asked for, but I think it is more realistic and more beneficial to both of us. Another point is, if we move out, what new tenant is going to be attracted by your 20% increase in the present economic climate? If your office lies empty, you will lose money! What do you think?*

Landlord: *Yes, this is indeed quite far from what I was hoping to achieve today, but I guess you have convinced me along the way that my 20% increase is too steep for the current situation, despite the fact we are also going through a rough patch ourselves. Having said that, we are also pretty hard-pressed to accept only 7% as our costs really have gone up significantly in real terms. In order to settle and put this behind us, may I suggest the following for us to consider: we will up this increase by another percentage point to 8%, and at the same time, we will extend the tenancy agreement from the current two years to four years! The rental for the first two years will be increased by 8%, and the second two years by a further 2%! Is this acceptable to you?*

Rep.: *Let me see if I have understood you. You are saying that if we agree to a 4-year tenancy term, then the first two years*

> *will be at a rental which is equal to an 8% increase from the*
> *current rental, and the rental for the second two years will*
> *be another 2%, i.e., 10%, more from the current rental. Is*
> *that the correct interpretation of what you have just said?*

Landlord: *Yes, exactly! Can we work with this?*

Rep.:   *Okay, I think we can probably accept this proposal. How-*
            ever, let me quickly check with our chairman first just to
            make sure that he is comfortable with a 4-year contract
            instead of a 2-year one, but I am pretty sure that he would
            be happy to comply with this request! I am glad that we have
            found a way to satisfy both of our needs, we look forward to
            working with you again. Thank you!

Landlord: *It's me who should say thank you!*

From the above example, we see that the representative has obviously made a plan; he has obviously set his objectives (rent he is prepared to pay) within a range; he states what he wants the negotiation to achieve; he recaps and clarifies what has been said; and he handles an unacceptable proposal politely and well.

Preparing for the Negotiation

If you consider a negotiation session as an examination, you will understand the value of being prepared. If you are well prepared, you raise the chances of success very much.

You may think that being prepared means learning all you can about the party that you will be negotiating with. Yes, this is important, but even more important is learning your own business thoroughly. The last thing you want is the other side teaching you what you should already know.

Write Your Preparations

On a piece of paper, list:

1. What your interests are, that is, what are motivating your wants? Why do you want what you want? By answering that question, you will uncover your interests.

2. The issues for negotiation, and what you want out of each issue. Finally, prioritize the wants on a high, medium or low scale. (Your wants may also be negative, i.e., what you do not want). High-scale wants are wants that you must have and will not negotiate under any circumstances. Medium-scale wants are wants that you intend to get, and may be open to some negotiation. Low-scale wants means wants that you would prefer to get but will negotiate. Put your wants together in a column. Establish a range rather than a fixed point for each want.

3. Your entry offers. This is the lowest you are prepared to offer the other side. Clarify also your exit offers — the maximum you are prepared to offer.

4. What you do not want, and also establish how much you do not want it. Try to think what the other side will want, what their entry and exit offers might be, and how they might prioritize their wants.

5. Any information you may have that would help you in the negotiation. List all the information that you do not want to disclose to the other side, especially not at the beginning of discussions. List the information that would be damaging to your case if you disclosed it to the other side. Make a list of all the information you will need during the negotiations to prove the assumptions you will have to make about the other side.

Make a plan for the negotiation. If it gets lost in the negotiations, or becomes inappropriate, have a back-up plan ready. Write everything down, and take it to the negotiating table with you.

Negotiating with Other Cultures

If you have to negotiate with someone from another culture, you can be assured that their techniques and way of negotiating will be very different from yours. When dealing with people in other countries, the biggest mistake you can make is to think that they are the foreigners. Nothing could be further from the truth: you are the foreign one, and you will have to adapt to their ways.

If dealing with people from other cultures in Hong Kong, keep in mind at all times that they will still behave as they would in their own country — they are not going to negotiate like Hong Kong Chinese just because they happen to be in Hong Kong!

In addition to the skills you will have to learn above, and the preparation you will have to make as also outlined above, you will have to learn everything you can about the behaviour of the other culture, in a business sense and otherwise. Learn how they negotiate, how they do business, learn their gestures and body language. For example, the Japanese have sixteen different ways of saying "no" so that the other side will not be offended by a refusal. If you do business with the Japanese, it will be worth learning what they are. If you learn as much as possible about the business and negotiating behaviour of the other side, you enter into negotiations with other cultures, you will not be surprised by anything they may say or do, and in addition, you will be able to respond to their ways appropriately.

Exercise I

A   Answer the following questions.

1. What is negotiation?
2. Give three examples of situations involving negotiation.
3. Who, do you think, are born masters of negotiation?
4. Why is negotiation essential in business and trade?
5. Why do people negotiate?
6. People negotiate so that they may benefit the other side. True or False?
7. In personal, everyday negotiations, what are the objectives of the people involved?
8. In business negotiations, what do top negotiators aim for? Why?
9. Why can negotiation be learned?
10. List the nine communication skills necessary in the art of negotiation.

B

An employee, Mr. Chan, is trying to negotiate with his department head, Mr. Cheung, for a salary increase. In Mr. Cheung's mind, Mr. Chan has performed acceptable work in the past, but does not warrant an increase mid-year.

Students are to act out the negotiation in class.

Before the negotiation, a pair of students is selected to act out the negotiation. Each of the pair is given the information, described below, that only he or she is supposed to know. One student will play Mr. Chan, and the other Mr. Cheung. Mr. Chan is anxious to increase his earnings because he feels he is doing some exceptional work, but his supervisor Mr. Cheung feels that the standards are barely acceptable. Mr. Cheung does not mind if Mr. Chan leaves the company but he does not wish that to happen soon, which could be the case if Mr. Chan does not get the increase that he is now seeking. Therefore, it is in Mr. Cheung's interests to have Mr. Chan stay for about one year. Mr. Cheung's challenge in this negotiation is to keep Mr. Chan with the company while not giving in to the request for an increase. Mr. Cheung is challenged to find out what would keep Mr. Chan to stay. As for Mr. Chan, while he really wants to have the increase, he realizes that the present economy is not good, and his employer may be unwilling to comply. He does not really want to leave unless he does not achieve anything with this negotiation. He would be satisfied for the time being if he gets either one of the following (failing a salary increase):

1. to have the company sponsor him for an evening class in order to improve his management skills; or
2. to set a list of performance targets for six months, and if he reaches these targets, then he will be promoted to a senior title as well as enjoying the salary compensation that goes with such a promotion.

C

This exercise is similar to B above, except that this time, Mr. Chan is a valuable asset to the company, so his department head definitely does not want Mr. Chan to leave. Mr. Cheung would normally be happy to comply with Mr. Chan's wish, but unfortunately, the department's budget has been tightly controlled recently because of the poor company results. Mr. Cheung is therefore unable to review any salary adjustments until the end of the year.

Mr. Chan, realizing the company is performing badly, knows that his chance of success is not great, but he does want his department head to know that he is not happy with the current situation, and that there are more offers out in the job market for him. However, he does enjoy his work, and unless he absolutely has to, he does not really want to depart. He would stay if the company agreed to either increase his salary per his request, or give him a promotion in title to "Senior Engineer" immediately, with a salary review to follow only at the end of the year.

D

A bank robber is holding a small branch bank manager hostage at the bank's premises. The robber demands a HK$2M ransom before he will release his hostage. The bank is surrounded by police, and a chief inspector has been tasked to negotiate with the robber for the release of the hostage.

The robber knows well that he has been surrounded, and there is no way he can get away alone; he has to have the hostage with him before he can make away safely. The robber's aim is to get away safely with the HK$2M, he is not interested in hurting anyone.

The aim of the police is to arrest the robber without paying out anything. As a general practice, they will not give in to demands from robbers, terrorists and the like. The Chief Inspector's job is to:

1. arrest the robber with force but with the minimum of casualties;
2. find a way to convince the robber to give himself up.

(The robber is not a professional, he has been driven to his crime because of the poor economy. He has been laid off recently by his employer, and finds himself without the money to support the education of his son — his only family member. The robber may give himself up when reminded he would not be able to support his son in any way if he hurts the hostage and ends up in prison for a long time.)

Exercise II

Find five faults in the following negotiation scenario where a negotiation did not go as smoothly and eventually it breaks down. One of the major reason for the breakdown in talks is the fact that the parties involved in the negotiation did not plan ahead and did not really have a negotiation plan prepared, and thus they did not know whether their limits were reached, and they were not effective in terms of giving proposals and counter-proposals.

The scenario is still the case of a representative of a company discussing with the landlord to lower the percentage increase for the office rental, where the latter is proposing a 20% increase.

Rep.: Mr. Leung, we have received your notification last week informing us that as starting from the next rental period, our rental for the office will be augmented by 20%. We feel this is ridiculous. Anyway, how can you do that?

Landlord: The reason we would like to have this amount of increase is because we have hardly increased at all during our last rental revision round. Now that the economy is bad and our costs are scaling up fast, we

	would like to bring our revenues more in line with our expenses.
Rep.:	I appreciate the fact that your costs might be going up quite dramatically especially with the frequent increases in interest rates recently, so your mortgage servicing costs must have gone up quickly. Having said that, you can't just put the rental up by a ridiculous 20% without regard to what is happening also in the market-place for office rentals! Are you aware that there are many vacant buildings around? I think we ought to be asking you for a rental reduction, never this 20% increase nonsense!
Landlord:	Yes, I realize that there are vacant office buildings around. There are always some vacant offices available even in the best of times, just as there are always some people who are unemployed. My belief is that this is a grade-A office building which is centrally located with easy access to many transportation means; I am convinced that its value is worth the 20% increase!
Rep.:	Unfortunately, we cannot see eye-to-eye here about its value, my opinion is that 20% increase is way too much. Unless you are going to modify this significantly, I don't think we can continue to do business — our alternative is obviously to move out when the current tenancy agreement expires in a few months' time; as there are numerous office space which are vacant, finding something suitable for us should not be a problem..
Landlord:	Are you saying that if I do not reduce the rate of increase, your company will move out of this office building when the present agreement expires in July?
Rep.:	Yes, that's exactly what I am saying!

Landlord: Have you given due consideration to the disruption this would do to your company and your business? Often just to be able to continue doing business without this sort of interruption is worth quite a lot! Isn't this worth the 20%?

Rep.: We realize the inconvenience of having to move, and I know it is probably worth something not having to change to another location, but I have no idea how much this is good for, may be it is worth 20%, may be more, may be less. How am I supposed to tell? However, I feel so strongly about this issue that I personally would rather have this inconvenience than agreeing to a proposal which I feel is unfair and ridiculous. I really think you have to change your proposal dramatically, otherwise we will just look for another office! I am sure you realize that it is also worth quite a lot too having a tenant that stays! In times like this, it is difficult for you to bring in other tenants so easily. What new tenant would pay all that rent? And if the office is left empty for a month or two, you would be back to where you are right now! What good would that do you?

Landlord: Mr. Chan, I don't really think our talk is going anywhere today, I believe we are too personally and emotionally wrapped up in this issue. May I suggest that we postpone this discussion for another week, we can then each do our homework before our next discussion; it may be more fruitful that way? What do you think?

Rep.: No, I would rather that we settle this today. I think it is wrong for you to ask for such an unfair increase in one go. It is a question of principle for me. So unless you back down quite a bit, I will call this talk closed and we will just go ahead to find another place!

Landlord: Okay, if this is how you feel and if this is the only possibility you think feasible, then let me grant you this wish. I will just go ahead and advertise for new tenants, and you can go ahead and look for your place. This office building is so centrally located, I don't think that this office space will go vacant for long. It is a pity that it has to end like this, but we thank you for your past business anyway.

Rep.:   Likewise, goodbye!

Task I

Split into groups of three. Imagine that you have been headhunted for an exciting new job with a new company. However, you live with your parents in Sheung Shui, very far from where your new office will be in Chai Wan. It will take you almost three hours to travel to work, and another three to get home again. Monthly transport expenses for you will be high. In addition, you will be working late very often and the last bus to your village runs at 7 p.m. in the evening, forcing you to take a taxi home, an $80 fare each time. Moving house to be closer to your place of work is impossible. You want to negotiate the terms of your contract to include travelling expenses for yourself to and from work.

The issue to be negotiated — travel expenses for you — is a very simple one. But the company may not want to agree to paying you extra for your travelling expenses because they feel that you will already be earning a good salary and your travel expenses should come out of it. The company may also feel it unfair to give one employee a travel allowance while all other employees have to pay for their own fares. On the other hand, you are a very promising young business person, and the company actually headhunted you because it feels you would be of great value to the company. You, however, feel so strongly about this issue that you have made up your mind to reject the job if the company does not agree to giving you a travel allowance.

But, if, during the negotiation, the company comes up with a compromise, will you accept? If you refuse, you risk losing the job of your dreams. If the company refuses, they will lose a good business person.

Two of your group represent the company, the other plays the role of the employee. Negotiate with particular emphasis on the skills learned.

Task II

Read through Task I exercise. Split into groups of three. One of you will be the promising young employee, the other two will represent the company.

At home, write out a simple plan for your negotiation. (The two company representatives are to each write their own plan, and confer and agree to a common plan in class).

8

Informal Reports

In this chapter, you will learn:
- how to gather data for an informal report;
- two methods of presenting date;
- how to write eight common types of informal report.

What Is an Informal Report?

You have already learned how to write memos. Memos are short internal messages; that is, they are sent to members of staff working in the same company or organization. Memos can be sent to the person at the next desk, or to a colleague in a subsidiary division of the company in other parts of the world.

In this chapter we will be looking at another kind of internal communication — the internal report; that is, a report which does not leave the company.

Reports, as the name suggests, report on action taken by an individual or individuals, and the outcome, if necessary. There are two basic kinds of reports. One is the formal report, which is meant to be read by an individual or individuals outside the company. Formal reports can also be used inside an organization to cover a subject in detail. The other, mentioned above, is the informal report, which is to be read only by an individual or individuals inside the company.

Internal reports are much longer than memos, usually a few pages.

Internal reports tend to be written informally, because only people working within the same company or organization will read them. Although internal reports are informally written, the techniques used to write them still have to be learned. Informal report writing is also an important managerial skill.

Different Kinds of Informal Reports

There are several kinds of informal reports which may be written for someone else within a company, depending on the information contained in them. Here they are:

1. *Data reports* — These reports gather together information or data. For example, they may present sales figures, on a daily, weekly, monthly or annual basis. They simply present data, no more.

2. *Suggestion reports* — Suggestion reports also display data, but, unlike data reports, suggestion reports suggest ways in which the data can be used for the benefit of the company. For example, if sales figures for a particular product line are low, then the suggestion can be made to drop that line from the stock. Suggestion reports are always requested. The writer will have been asked to look into the sales figures for that particular product line and report them, giving suggestions.

3. *Reason reports* — Reason reports are similar to suggestion reports because they recommend that a certain action be taken. But for reason reports, the writer is not asked to present the report. The writer does it himself or herself. The writer looks into a specific area, reports what he or she sees, and suggests a solution.

4. *Progress reports* — If an out-of-the-ordinary event is going to happen in a company, a progress report will tell the management the progress being made by the company to meet that event. For example, if Bill Gates is to visit the factories in China making his software in one year's time, a progress report will keep the management informed of the company's preparations for his visit, for example, if the preparations are running smoothly, if changes to the planning are needed, and what the next steps in the planning will be.

5. ***Proposal reports*** — A proposal is an outline written by an individual or an organization stating what he or she or it can do for a company to benefit it. Proposal reports are asked for by the company. For example, if a company is in trouble, it may invite consultants from several different consulting firms to solve the problem. The consultants would then each submit a proposal report to the company, explaining how he or she would solve the problem. The consultant who writes the best proposal report will be hired for the job.

6. ***Meeting reports*** — What is said during meetings has to be recorded in writing. This written recording is called the Minutes of the meeting, and can be regarded as a report. Meeting reports (Minutes) are taken during the meeting, usually by a secretary, and typed up neatly within 12 hours. Minutes can be taken for meetings which take place regularly or irregularly.

7. ***Precis reports*** — Precis are summaries. Precis reports summarize data, proposals, recommendations, or simply long reports of any kind. You may remember being asked to write a precis at school — shortening a long paragraph down to two or three sentences giving the main basic ideas.

8. ***File reports*** — Sometimes, conversations, ideas or actions are important enough to record in writing. When they have been written down, they must be filed, and so such reports are called file reports. These days, there are many different methods of communication, and communications fly fast and furious between individuals, and companies. What was said or not said, what was done or not done, ideas that were mentioned, etc., any of which may be of great importance in the future, go into a file report.

Layouts of Reports

Reports can be written like letters, using a letter layout. However, unlike a letter, this kind of report will be a lot more structured, with great use of headings etc. When the report is informal, the letter layout is suitable.

Reports can also be written like memos. This kind of layout can be used if many people in the company are going to read it. The headings at the top of this kind of report are the same as the ones you would use for a memo. Memo forms can even be used. Again, the memo format is used when the report is an informal one.

Reports also have their own kind of layout — used for longer, more formal, official reports.

Reports can also be written on a standard form which has already been printed. Here, the information required goes into the blank spaces. These are useful for events that are common and regular within an organization — for example lost property report forms, or police eye-witness reports.

In the days before computers, reports were laboriously typed. Now, for a report to look truly professional, a computer is a must, and as well as learning the skills necessary for writing reports, you must also learn the computer and word-processing skills necessary for presenting your report to the reader in a professional way. Further on in this chapter, we will be looking at the most effective ways to present reports.

An informal report should be short and concise

Structuring the Informal Report

Which layout will you use for your report? When you know why you are writing the report, and you know who will read it, you will know what layout to use.

Before you begin to write your report, you must ask yourself why you are writing it. Are you writing it to inform someone, or to propose action to someone, or to make a suggestion? Or are you writing it simply as an exercise to sharpen your writing skills? The purpose of writing your report should be clear in your head before you begin. Write down the purpose of writing the report on a piece of paper to clarify it for yourself. For example, the manager of an up-market fashion retail outlet may write: "I am writing this report in order to present the February sales figures of the 'Comme des Garcons' garment range."

After you have established why you are writing the report, the next thing to clarify in your mind is the person or people who will be reading your report.

If the person who will read your report is familiar with the background of what you are doing, you will not have to include details to explain it. If, on the other hand, the person who is to read your report is unfamiliar with your work, you will have to supply background information to him or her.

The person or people who will be reading your report will, obviously, influence the style of your writing, the vocabulary you use, and the way you put your ideas across. You also need to know how the reader will use your report, and aim your report so that the reader will be able to use it easily.

Collecting the Information

The next step is to thoroughly collect all the information you need for your report and to check this data to make sure that it is accurate. If your report is to be credible, obviously you must get all the facts right.

Arranging the Information

Informal reports may be laid out using either the direct or the indirect method. You will remember that, with the direct method, the main idea is mentioned first, followed by supporting explanations and reasons. With the indirect method, reasons and explanations are given first, followed by the main idea. In reports, use the indirect method if you want to persuade the reader, or if the reader does not have much knowledge of what you are writing about. If the reader is not familiar with the subject of your report, the indirect method will inform him or her first. Use the direct method when writing reports if the reader is familiar with the subject of your report, because he or she will want to get to the main idea quickly. In general, reports are written using the direct method. This is because in general, reports in business are written to inform, and their readers will be neutral or pleased on reading them.

Keeping Your Emotions and Feeling Out of Reports

When writing reports, you must be objective. This means that you must present only the cold facts, which are free of your opinion, and you must write so that the reader will have no idea how the information makes you feel, or what it makes you think. Present the information in factual language, and, if you are quoting from another source, always be sure to mention the exact details of that source. Never criticize another person or organization in a report. Keep your opinion out of it.

Headings in Your Reports

Throughout your report, use headings. They will make you, the writer, organize your writing into related sections of information. They will help the reader to more clearly understand the presentation of your information.

Keep your headings short and clear. Try to make your headings "summarize" what you write in the paragraph(s) following it. There is no need to use quotation marks with headings. Make them stand out from the rest of the text. For example, on a computer you can make them bold and underline them.

Below is a description and explanation of each of the eight different kinds of reports. In the given examples of the different kinds of reports, memo format is used, with the exception of the proposal report. As mentioned above, memo format is perfectly acceptable for informal, internal reports.

Data Reports

As mentioned at the beginning of this chapter, data reports simply convey data to the reader. Some data reports can be written on a standard form, like police eyewitness reports, lost property reports, or college progress reports. Data reports can also be more individualized, where the whole report is written out by the sender. If a data report is to be written out in full, then it must be divided into relevant sections. These sections are:

1. the beginning, or the introduction,
2. the body, or the information, and
3. the conclusion, or the summary.

The ***beginning*** of a data report tells the reader why you are writing the report, and also details the methods used to collect the data. The beginning of a data report also states that the data is accurate and gives proof to back up your statement. The beginning will also give any other information that might be relevant to the report.

The ***body*** of the data report gives the information you want to present to the reader. It is important that you present this data attractively, and also logically, in a format that makes it easy for the reader to understand quickly. An attractive layout is very pleasing to the eye, and makes your report look professional. This is where word-processing skills are useful. If you find that the data needs explanation(s), it is better to put the explanation(s) in a later section and label this section "Discussion."

The ***conclusion*** is usually unnecessary in a data report. As mentioned above, a data report simply presents data, nothing more, and so there is nothing to conclude at the end. However, you may like to round off your report with a sentence about the data. It is permissible to give here a brief summary of the data you have presented. Try to make it no longer than one sentence, and state simply the facts.

Here is an example of an informal data report:

✍

To: Mrs. L. Huang
From:
Date:
Subject: SALES FIGURES FOR THE "COMME DES GARCONS" GARMENT
         RANGE, MARCH–JULY 1998

These figures are accurate, and are taken from the XXX. They are represented in Hong Kong dollars.

Range	March	April	May	June	July
Comme des Garcons	150,876	122,985	128,653	108,923	106,999

Suggestion Reports

Suggestion reports both present data to the reader, like data reports, but they also suggest to the reader ways to improve or remedy the situation. They make recommendations. Usually, suggestion reports are requested. This means that a boss will ask an employee to present such a report to him or her.

Suggestion reports can be written using either the direct or the indirect method. If you use the direct method, state your suggestion or conclusion near the beginning of the report. If you use the indirect method, state your suggestion or conclusion towards the end. Use the indirect method if you feel that you will have to persuade the reader, that is, if you feel that the reader will resist your suggestions and recommendations.

Here is an example of an informal suggestion report:

✍

To: Mrs. L. Huang
From:
Date:
Subject: SALES FIGURES, "COMME DES GARCONS" MARCH–JULY 1998,
         WITH RECOMMENDATION

This report is in response to your request to outline the sales figures for the

"Comme des Garcons" garment range for the months of March–July 1998. These figures are accurate, and are taken from the XXX. They are represented in Hong Kong dollars. A recommendation for the low July figure, also requested, follows.

Range	March	April	May	June	July
Comme des Garcons	150,876	122,985	128,653	108,923	106,999

Sales figures for this range fell by XX% in July 1998. I recommend that in future the spring collection be delivered in February or March at the latest, ready for display in March or April. Having a winter collection still available in April, when the weather is too warm for these garments, is the reason for the low sales figures for that month.

Reason Reports

Reason reports are very similar to suggestion reports. They present data and suggest ways to the reader to improve or remedy the situation. However, the only real difference is that nobody asks the writer of reason reports to write the report! We learned that a boss would ask a subordinate for a suggestion report. With reason reports, the writer has the idea to write to report. The writer would present data, would explain the data and would make a recommendation based on the data to improve a situation. For example, the writer might see a reason to buy a product that would be of benefit to the company, such as a laserjet colour printer, or a drinks machine. The writer would start by suggesting the need for such a machine, and then explain the need for such a product, giving his or her reasons for suggesting it. Or the writer might want to change, for example, some department policy. He or she might think that the present clocking-in/clocking-out system is unnecessary. The writer would start by suggesting the disposal of the policy, and then give his or her reasons for his or her statements, based on the data presented in the report.

Reason reports are usually written using the direct method — that is, the suggestion is given first, followed by the reasons for making the suggestion, in the form of data.

Reason reports can be split into three or four headed sections:

"Suggestion," "Present Situation," and "Benefits of Suggestion." A fourth heading, if appropriate, could be "Financial Benefit" if the suggestion will save the company money. Here is an example of a reason report:

✍🏻

To: Mr. Lo
From:
Date:
Subject: ACQUISITION OF BUBBLEJET LASER COLOUR PRINTERS IN GRAPHICS DEPARTMENT

Suggestion

I propose the acquisition of two more bubblejet laser printers for the Graphics Department.

Present Situation

Because there are three graphic artists now working full-time in the Graphics Department, each of us finds that we are having to wait for the one colour printer available to us. This waiting time can be long (up to two hours), and, I feel, totally unproductive, as we cannot be getting on with what we have to do until we can print.

Benefits of Suggestion

If each member of staff were to have his or her own printer, there would no longer be any waiting time, and the department would operate more productively as a result.

Financial Benefit

Although costly, increased department productivity would offset the cost of the two printers within a short period of time.

Progress Reports

Progress reports show the progress made by a department or a company to meet unusual future events. For example, a company might want to participate in an annual international trade fair in Europe, where the latest products will be on display. As far as perhaps a year or even more before the event, the appropriate department(s) will start planning for the fair. A progress report will keep the upper management informed of what is being done within the company to meet the event on time.

Progress reports are composed of four sections. The first part of a progress report reminds the reader of why the report is being written. The second part tells the reader briefly what has been done up to date to meet the future event. The third part of a progress report gives full details of any preparations which are happening at the present time, and the fourth part gives any preparations and suggestions which will be made in the future for the event to come, in view of its date. Here is an example of a progress report:

✍

To: R. K. Ho
From:
Date: 18th September 1997
Subject: PROGRESS OF FACTORY IN CHINA

Review

From 1st January to the present day, the site at Panyu has been developed well within schedule, despite the hold-up in February due to an influenza epidemic among the builders. The factory should be fully operational on our projected date of 1st April 1998, and to date we are well on target for then.

Past Progress

Construction began on 1st January of this year with the mapping out and laying of foundations. This was completed on 18th May and wall and flooring constructions are ongoing to date.

Present Situation

Continuation with wall and flooring construction in accordance with architect's plans. The construction of a driveway off the main highway, and a large parking area to the west side of the factory are now at present under way.

Future Schedule

Continued construction of the walls and flooring, followed by the roofing is envisaged until the 31st of December 1997. Between the end of December and the end of February 1998, windows, and wall and flooring finishings are expected, as well as wiring and plumbing. From the end of February until the end of March, decoration is expected, followed by the furnishing of the premises, in time for full occupancy on 1st April.

Proposal Reports

A proposal report usually offers a service to a company or a department. It must persuade the reader to use the writer's proposed service, and it does this by trying to convince the reader that the service offered is needed, and indeed is the best on the market. If the service is offered to solve a problem, usually the writer will give an explanation of the strategy he or she intends to use to solve the problem. Proposal reports are usually solicited — this means that someone asks the writer for the report.

An example is a company with a problem. If the company has never before used the services of a consultant, the company may then approach several consulting firms to see how each proposes to solve the problem. Each consultant would submit his or her individual proposal report, outlining exactly what steps he or she would take to solve the problem. The company would choose the consultant whose proposal report was liked best.

Proposal reports are usually divided into six sections. The first section is the ***introduction***. If the proposal report was asked for (solicited), the introduction will remind the reader why the report was requested. If the proposal report was not asked for (unsolicited), the introduction will state the reasons for the proposal to the reader. Also in the introduction will be the writer's credibility, that is, a few sentences to tell the reader that the writer is well-qualified and/or experienced enough to be able to handle the problem easily.

As mentioned above, proposal letters are persuasive. Whatever the reason behind a proposal letter, the writer wants the reader to buy what is on offer. In the introduction, writers will mention something which will grab the attention of the reader and arouse his or her interest. This "something" could be:

- a mention of very good past results,
- a guarantee of an attractive price,
- a promise of a fast solution,
- a hint that well-known corporations use your services,
- a hint that the writer can easily solve the problem.

The second section in a proposal report is called the ***challenge***. It mentions the purpose of the proposition by isolating the problem. If the proposal report has not been requested by an organization, the writer must make the reader believe that there really is a problem to be fixed. This is done by detailing the problem. If the proposal report has been requested (solicited), the writer may copy many of the words and phrases used by the company in their original communication asking for the proposal report. This brings the problem more firmly and clearly to the attention of the company, and it also shows the company asking for the proposal report that the writer would be familiar with the problem. In a short proposal, the introduction and the challenge can be written in the same section.

The third section of a proposal report is called the ***proposal***. In this section, the writer proposes a solution to the problem. In the proposal, the writer is actually selling his or her services, so this part of the proposal report can be considered to be much like a sales letter. The writer explains how he or she intends to solve the problem, explaining why the reader should choose his or her services (perhaps as opposed to the services proposed by competitors), detailing the benefits the reader will enjoy, including "after sales" service, if appropriate.

The fourth section of a proposal report is known as ***staff***. In this section, the writer gives details of any other person or people who would be working on the problem, and of their track record (their experience, qualifications, previous success record, etc.).

The fifth section of the proposal report is the ***cost***. This section gives details of how much your services will cost the reader should he or she hire you. You should give yourself a margin here in case your costs increase unexpectedly while working on the project, yet you do not want to be too expensive. In this section too, you should give the reader a date by which you would like an answer.

The final section of a proposal report is known as the ***acceptance***. This section asks the reader to take action, much as a sales letter does, and also asks for a deposit to secure the business. As the reader may be considering several proposals, it will be necessary in this section to tell him or her that you will be withdrawing your proposal after a certain date. This is so that if you do not hear from the reader by that date, you can assume that he or she will not be taking up your sevices. It also prompts the reader to act if he or she is interested in your proposal.

Proposal reports are not usually written in memo format because they come from an outside source. If, however, the proposal is an internal one, then memo format is perfectly acceptable. Here is an example of a proposal report, showing all the six sections above.

21st November 1998

Dear Mr. Lin,

I very much enjoyed spending last Monday to Wednesday speaking with the functional heads of all the departments of your company, at your request. I understand from our meetings that you have serious concerns about the long-term viability of your firm. (1)

After a first analysis, I can see that there are indeed critical areas of non-performance which need to be corrected without further delay.

One area of concern is the lax attitude shown by the credit department in collecting payments, thus exacerbating an already severely strained cash flow stream. Our company specializes in financial re-engineering and marketing planning, and has had over 15 years of turning round companies with similar symptoms to that of yours. Many of our clients have since become the market leaders of their field, and we like to think that we have had a hand in helping this happen. (2)

From my meeting with your staff last week, it is clear to me that they are seriously out of line with the vision of the company. Also the company is in critical need of truly innovative products if it is to regain lost market shares and to enhance profitability. The company's cash flow problem comes from three main sources:

1. A "me-too" product strategy severely undermining profit margins;
2. Excessively long credit terms needed to secure business because of the unattractiveness of the products themselves; and
3. Lack of discipline in enforcing the trade terms and collecting receivables due. (3)

These problems may sound difficult but are fairly easy to resolve. It is very much our objective to be a partner of your company to rectify these issues, and to see to it that your firm returns to a strong cash position and a much-strengthened balance sheet within 18 months. To achieve this goal, we will* need to work with you over this 18-month period. Initially, we will* need to conduct an analysis of the industry that you serve, followed by an in-depth company investigation. These two steps will require two months each, after which a detailed report will* be submitted with our findings and recommendations. After these four months, you may let us know whether you would like us to continue based on the quality of our report. If you should choose to stop at this point, you will* only be charged 50% of the total fee. Once you decide to continue, we will* then enter the second phase — that of implementing strategy and tactics. The estimated total number of hours will* be approximately 2,000 man-hours of consulting and analytical work. (4)

I will* be the person overseeing this project. However, most of the investigative and analytical work will* be carried out by Stanley Hong, our Senior Consultant, and Peter Fong, Associate Consultant. Stanley Hong has been with us for over 12 years and is a recognized leader in strategic marketing, whereas Peter Fong is a recent addition to our team. He has an MBA from Harvard Business School in the United States with a specialization in finance. I am confident that you will* be satisfied with the professionalism and the world of knowledge these two gentlemen will* bring to the table. (5)

Our professional fee for seeing this project to completion is* HK$600,000, plus extras for travels, sundry expenses and accommodation on an actual usage basis. To reflect our confidence in resolving your problems, we are prepared to receive our fees as follows:

1. Deposit of $10,000 on acceptance.
2. Two-thirds to be paid on a monthly basis per time accumulated at an hourly rate of HK$200 per man-hour.
3. The balance, one-third, less deposit, to be paid after the company returns to net profitability of at least 5%. (6)

If our proposal agrees with your expectations, please return the enclosed consent form, along with a deposit cheque for $10,000 as confirmation of your acceptance. Please note that the details in this proposal are valid until 31st December only. (7)

Yours sincerely,

Albert Ma
Partner
Johnston Gilmore Co. Ltd.

Note that in (1), the writer gives the introduction and it states a reminder of why the proposal was requested. In (2), the writer grabs the reader's attention by mentioning his past successes with other major companies. The writer then isolates the problem in (3) and puts forward the proposal in (4). The writer mentions the staff who will be working with him in (5), giving their experience and qualifications. The cost is given in (6) and in the final section (7), the writer closes the sale with a request for acceptance.

Note also the language the writer uses in this proposal. Usually in a proposal, the conditional tense is used. For example, a consultant might write: "if you agreed to hiring us for the task, we would do X, we would do Y, and we would do Z." The tense used is the conditional with "would," because at this stage in the process the proposal has not been accepted. But in the above example of a proposal report, the consultant uses the word "will" — we will do X, Y and Z, as shown by *. This is a clever language tactic, because it puts the idea into the mind of the reader that this consultant will be the one for the job. The word "will" is much more assertive than "would," which is why the writer uses it.

Also in the cost, the writer says that the amount "is" $600,000, and not the amount "would be" $600,000 for the same reasons.

Meeting Reports

"Minutes" is the name for the written report of what was said in a meeting, including conclusions and action to follow, if any.

Formal minutes for large companies give the exact wording of what was said in the meeting; sometimes written from a recording of the meeting. Informal reports give much less detail than formal reports. Informal reports outline briefly what was said, conclusions drawn, and action to follow. You will learn how to write minutes for meetings in Chapter 10. However, here is an example of informal minutes:

✍

TONG CHEE KWA VILLAGE OWNERS' COMMITTEE
Minutes of Meeting held on 16th June 1998 at 8 p.m. at the Residents Club

Present: Mr. Kevin Choi (KC) — Chairperson

Ms. Valerie So (VS) — Vice-Chairperson

Mr. Tommy Chu (TC) — Member

Mr. Leung Luk-cheng (LLC) — Member

Mr. Daniel Kwok (DK) — Member

Mr. Alex Cho (AC) — Assistant Estate Manager, City Management

Mr. Patrick Lui (PL) — Senior Estate Officer, City Management

Ms. Wanda Chan (WC) — Assistant Community Relations Officer,
City Management

Apologies: Mr. Cheung Chi-woo

Mr. Paul Fong

Mr. Eric Sung

Ms. Ting So Lung

In Attendance: Mrs. Kwong on behalf of Mr. Eric Sung

1. Confirmation of the Minutes of the Last Meeting

Minutes of the Annual General meeting and the Inaugural Meeting 97/98 held on 22nd April 1998, were confirmed.

2. New Business

2.1 Corridor Lighting

In response to the Committee's enquiry about the progress of the replacement of the dim corridor lights, City Management replied that the lights would be replaced upon delivery of new lights in mid-August. City Management will keep a spare supply as suggested by members.

2.2 Cable TV

Regarding negotiations with Wharf Cable, Mr. Tommy Chu, member of the COC Sub-Committee on Satellite & Cable TV, explained that eight more channels would be added to the SMCTV system and this preliminary agreement would be sent to a solicitor for comment. City Management will release a management notice if the final agreement is approved.

2.3 Landscape

City Management has agreed to plant more greenery around houses numbers 18 and 19. City management will cut the long grass beside the road leading to the car park.

2.4 Blocked Drains

Mr. Tommy Chu found that the drains under the steps of houses numbers 1 and 2 are always blocked when it rains and flooding is the result. City

Management will install wire netting in the drains to catch leaves and debris. The situation should improve.

2.5 Rollerskating in Public Areas

Mr. Daniel Kwok asked whether City Management would take any measures to stop rollerskaters from skating in public areas. City Management replied that skaters were already banned from the areas of the bus station, the Residents' Club and in other busy areas that might cause an accident. When the security guards spotted skaters in these areas, they would be stopped.

3. Any Other Business

3.1 Resignation of Mr. Leung Luk-cheng from the Committee

Mr. Kevin Choi on behalf of the Committee thanked Mr. Leung for his contributions to the Committee.

4. Date of Next Meeting

The next meeting will be held on Monday, 25th August 1998, at 8.00 p.m., at the SunDown Restaurant in the Residents' Club.

As there was no other business, the meeting closed at 9.25 p.m.

Precise Reports

A precis is a brief summary of a long report. Some reports are indeed very long, and you may have to give just the main ideas, so that another or others in the organization can quickly understand the most important points without having to read the whole document. A precis normally covers just the main idea, leaving out anything else. The layout is important for quick and simple understanding, and facts may have to be numbered for easier reading. Here is an example of a precis report. This is a precis of the proposal report given above.

✍

To: Mr. John Chan — The Managing Director, Appleton Electric
From: David Lin
Date: 22nd November 1998
Subject: PROPOSAL LETTER FROM JOHNSTON GILMORE CO.

Albert Ma submitted his proposal yesterday. He mentioned that three critical problems have been identified:

1. staff mis-alignment with company vision,
2. non-competitive products that lack innovation,
3. abuse of credit terms and lax receivable collection practices.

Albert Ma proposed an 18-month project with us, the work to be carried out by two well-qualified consultants with backgrounds in strategic marketing and finance. Ma will oversee this project himself. The consultative work will comprise an analysis of our industry and an in-depth investigation of Appleton Electric, which will each take two months. A report will be submitted at the end of these four months with their findings and recommendations for improvements. We may cancel the project at that point if we do not agree with their findings or solutions; a 50% payment of the total fee would be due. The next step proposed is the implementation of the recommended solutions. A deposit of $10,000 is to be paid upon acceptance. The total fee will be HK$600,000, two-thirds of which is to be paid on a monthly basis based on the time accumulated at the rate of $200 per hour, and the balance of one-third minus deposit to be paid only after our company returns to net profitability of 5% or above.

The above proposal is valid only until 31st December.

File Reports

File reports are written in case the subject matter will be important in the future. For example, a conversation which results in a decision may be written as a file report. The conversation may have to be located in the future for some reason. For this reason it is important to write file reports as soon as possible after the event they are describing, or sometimes even during it, so that no part of the conversation is altered or forgotten. File reports are normally only made for important situations.

The file report contains all the names and titles of the people who took part in the conversation/decision etc. A copy of the file report is then sent to all the people involved in the report so that they may make changes to it as they see is necessary. When this is done, the report is typed up and filed. A copy of the final version is sent to all concerned. Here is an example of a file report. In this example, a manager has tried to tell a female employee that he will have to terminate her, because she is pregnant. Although this is illegal, she does not mention it in her file report. The file report simply states what was said. The legality of the case will be taken up elsewhere.

✍️

To: Mr. J. P. Wong
From: Ms. R. T. Tan
Date: 28th January 1998
Subject: TERMINATION OF EMPLOYMENT DUE TO PREGNANCY

This is to put in writing our conversation of this afternoon where you stated that I would have to leave my employ with you on Friday, 13th March of this year, because of my pregnancy. I understand that you wish to employ another person permanently in my place and I note therefore that you also stated that you do not wish me to take up my position with the company after the birth of my baby.

Please reply to me on or before Friday, 3rd of February if anything I have recorded in this memo to you is untrue.

Professionalize Your Presentations

As mentioned earlier, reports look much more professional if they are properly presented. With the abundance of computers now, there is no excuse for badly presented reports. Formal reports must look very professional. But even informal reports need to look their best. Here are some ways to get your reports looking first-class:

1. Use typeface size point 10.
2. Use the New York, Times or Helvetica font.
3. Do not square up right-hand margins. Uneven right hand margins make the document easier to read.
4. Leave a double space between paragraphs. Type two spaces between sentences.
5. For effective headings, use Helvetica bold capitals.
6. When you have finished your report, print it out and hold it away from you at arm's length. Try to see it as a work of art. Is the black and white balanced? Is the total text well balanced on the page? Not too squashed all at the top? Are the left and right margins wide enough? Top and bottom margins? If you have data or an illustration to present, make sure to put it a little above the centre of the page.

7. Aim for a simple-looking report. Do not kill it with too many headings, bold formats for emphasis, italics, capitals and underlinings.

Exercise I

A Name the eight different types of reports. Describe a situation where each would be required.

B Here are several situations. Say which kind of report would be most appropriate for each situation.

1. You have to present the month's sales figures to your boss.
2. You have to present the month's sales figures and suggest a solution to the problem of falling sales figures for product X.
3. You see that your department would greatly benefit from an extra colour photocopier.
4. The president of the company is coming from the United States to visit the company in 18 months' time.
5. You are a consultant who has been approached by a company with a problem.
6. You are asked to make a written record of a sales meeting.
7. Your boss asks you to list the main points in a very long report.
8. There is a conversation between yourself and a customer suggesting joint-venture in a manufacturing plant in China.
9. Your company will attend an international trade fair in the spring of next year.
10. You strongly feel that recruiting two extra sales executives will be of great advantage to your department.

C How are reason reports and proposal reports the same? How are they different?

D How is a reason report like a sales letter? How is it different?

Exercise II

Each member in the class is to approach companies around Hong Kong and ask to be given/sent/faxed a report that they will not mind you using for your communications course. Speaking to companies will sharpen your communication skills! You will use these in Task I below.

Task I

Split into pairs. If the class is an odd number, one group can be of three students. Bring your company reports into class, and put all the reports together. There should be about 10–20 reports in total. Give each report a number, and photocopy so that each pair has every report.

In your pairs, decide what kind of report each one is. Also write very briefly the situation it describes. For example: "Report Number 3. Progress Report. Reports on the progress of Supercompany in preparation for CEO's visit in March 1999." When each pair has completed every report, teacher goes through each report, number by number. Does the class agree on what kind of report it is? On what it describes? If there is disagreement, discuss in class.

Task II

A   Write a short reason report based on the following situation.

You notice that a certain situation can be improved in your department.

B   Write a short suggestion report based on the following situation.

Your boss is very impressed by your sales skills. He or she asks you to submit a report on the last six months' sales figures, and asks you to suggest a way to rectify the poor sales situation on a colleague's figures.

C   Write a short progress report based on the following situation.

Your rich uncle has lent you a great amount of money to attend a 2-year MBA course in Paris, on the condition that you do well in the course. You are now half way through the course and he asks you to submit a progress report on how you are doing in relation to your graduation in one years's time. Write a brief progress report for him.

9

Formal Reports

In this chapter, you will learn:
- where to collect data;
- where to research for your report;
- how to write purpose statements for your reports;
- how to present data effectively;
- how to lay out your report professionally.

What Is a Formal Report?

In the last chapter, you learned how to write informal reports. We saw that informal reports are most usually internally sent; that is, they stay within the company or organization.

Formal reports, on the other hand, are usually sent to people outside a company or organization. For this reason, they are written much more formally than internal reports; they are laid out traditionally; and they are much longer than informal reports.

Formal reports in business nowadays are in fact rather common. Their purpose is important — companies make major decisions based on the data and information in formal reports.

In this chapter you will learn how to collect the data and information needed for a formal report, how to organize it, and how to write and professionally present it.

Before You Start to Write

Formal reports, like informal ones, start by getting clear in your mind just why you are writing the report. You must have it clear in your mind what information and data you are going to include, and what you are not going to include. You need to know the deadline for your report, and the length it will be (in pages or words). What data will be necessary to include? Will it be easy to collect the data necessary for the report? How much detail should you include? How big should your sample(s) be, if you have to provide statistical data? All these factors should be clear in your head before you start to write.

Once you are clear about what you are writing about and are also clear about what to include and what not to include in the report, how long to make it, etc., you should first write a purpose statement. This simply states the aim of the report, its importance and its restrictions, that is, what is not covered in the report. A purpose statement is mainly just for your own reference. It will keep you "on track" as you are writing your report. However, it will also be of use should any body request the purpose of your report. Here is an example of a purpose statement:

The purpose of this report is to investigate the growing rate of obesity among Hong Kong schoolchildren aged 5 to 16. The results of this report will have far-reaching implications for parents, teachers and medical and health workers involved with children in Hong Kong. This report covers a sample of 80 Hong Kong government schools only.

Gathering Data

All reports are based on accurate data. For any report to be credible, it is very important that your data is one hundred per cent accurate. You can collect data from two kinds of sources — first-hand and second-hand. First-hand data is data collected from your own experiences and ob-servations. Second-hand data is data collected from other sources, for example from people who have had first-hand experiences. For example, if you are writing a report on UFO sightings, and you yourself have seen a UFO, that would be classed as first-hand data. However if you use an already published paper on UFO sightings, that would be classed as second-hand data.

First-hand Sources

The most important data for formal reports comes from first-hand sources. First-hand data is data which has never been collected, recorded and presented before. Some examples of first-hand sources are:

1. *Personal observation* — Personal observation is data recorded from what you see with your own eyes, for example, overweight children themselves.
2. *Interviews* — By asking people questions and logging their answers, you can collect first-hand data. Interviews tend to be lengthy.
3. *Surveys* — Similar to interviews but much shorter, a sample of the population is asked the same set of questions. The responses are logged, providing first-hand data.
4. *Experiments* — Conducting experiments yourself and analysing the results is another source of first-hand data.

Second-hand Sources

Second-hand data is data which has already been collected, recorded and presented by somebody else. It is found in (1) published papers, (2) newspaper and journal articles and periodicals, (3) computerized information and (4) reference books. These sources can provide excellent background information of what has already been compiled in the way of information and data on your topic. Your report will normally be presenting a new conclusion based on your findings. Second-hand sources provide old information which you can use as a general background to your work.

1. *Published papers* — If another person has previously researched and presented your topic in a published report, you may use this as background information, or, at the very least, as an overview of past research and findings available.

2. *Newspaper and journal articles, and periodicals* — These second-hand sources usually publish the most recent research covered and are useful for this reason. You can use them as an overview of activity to date before your own report which will present the latest findings.

3. *Computerized information* — Huge amounts of information is now stored on computer which may be accessed by anyone requiring information. These are called databases, and, as their name suggests, they store data. Databases search out data with extreme speed, and can contain vast stores of information. For these reasons, computerized information is fast becoming the principal source of second-hand data today.

4. *Reference books* — These are dictionaries, encyclopaedias, and the like. They often provide material which is relevant and useful to someone preparing a formal report.

Gathering Second-hand Data

Most writers of reports use second-hand sources as a background to their work. Material that has been published already, and the conclusions drawn from it, will give your report credibility. Using your local library should give you the information you need. Make the librarian your friend. Tell him or her what you are looking for and what you need. Ask the librarian to show you what resources the library stocks, and learn about them. Learn how to access them. Ask the librarian to show you if you are not sure. Once you have sources in your hands:

- Select only what you need to put your point across — you cannot use everything that has ever been written about your subject.
- Take good notes.

Quoting References

You must mention in your report all the data that you use from second-hand sources. You can put this information at the foot of the page as footnotes or at the end of each chapter as endnotes. You must also write down the title, author and publisher of every source you use. This is called the bibliography. The bibliography is listed in alphabetical order, usually at the end of a report.

Arranging the Formal Report

You need to be able to present your information and data in a clear, logical, readable way. Formal reports can be organized using the same principles as for informal reports. Think carefully about the kind of material you are presenting. How can it be organized? What sections can it be divided into for clear, logical presentation? In what order should the different sections be presented? What should be mentioned first? Next? Last? Will your report upset or offend the reader? Will the reader's reaction be neutral or positive?

You will remember that informal reports are usually written using the direct method of communication (stating the main idea first, followed by supporting, detail sentences). Formal reports can also be written using the direct method. In fact, if the reader knows about the subject of your report, the direct method is best. If the reader is not familiar with the subject of your report, the indirect method will be more effective (reasons and explanations first, main idea last). As you know, you would also use the indirect method if you think that your report will upset or offend the reader.

Reports make more sense if they are written in time order. This means presenting the events in the order in which they occurred, usually from the earliest to the most recent.

Think also of the space order of your report. If you mention geographical regions in your report, think of how to present them in a logical, readable order.

Sections of a Formal Report

As well as organizing the information and data of your report into logical, readable order, you must organize your report into logical sections. Usually there are between four and seven sections, with appropriate headings. An example of these headings might be:

Introduction → Problem (if any) → Past Findings →Method → Present Findings → Discussion → Conclusion

Some of these headings may be subtitles.

Making a Plan

It is essential that you, as the writer of a report, make a rough draft of your report before you begin to write it. On paper or on computer, write your headings, and organize your information and data under the headings in clear, logical order. As this is just a rough draft, change it as much as necessary until you like the look of it. Mark in the places where you would present charts, tables, graphs etc. Continue to work with your plan while writing your final version.

Charts, Tables and Graphs

Charts, tables and graphs are called visual aids and they are important for the reader in his or her assimilating and understanding of your data. Charts, tables and graphs are much more speedy and simple to read than the same information written in words. Give your visual aids titles or headings, and discuss them in the text above, alongside or underneath the part of the page where they appear. Present your visual data vertically down the page, that is, try to avoid presenting your charts, tables and graphs horizontally, so that the reader has to turn the page around to read the data. Always remember to mention the origin of the source if you are using second-hand data in your report.

The Final Report

Before the Report Begin

Formal reports have a formal format, even before the writing of the report begins. When the reader takes the formal report into his or her hands, the first page he or she will see is what is known as the "title fly

Charts, tables, figures can make presentation lively

page." On this page is simply the title of the report. It should be well thought-out, so that the subject of the contents is very clear to the reader. The second page of the report is called the "title page," and shows not only the title as in the title fly page, but also the full name of the writer, the company or organization who asked for the report, the name of the person or body who will read the report, and the date.

The third page of a report, known as the "terms of reference," suggests to the reader how the report should be read, mentions what it covers and what it does not cover, and suggests also how it may be considered and followed up. A table of contents may follow this, on another page. A summary of the entire work may or may not follow the contents. Finally, the report itself will begin.

Structuring the Report Itself

1. Introduction

A formal report will usually begin with an introduction. The introduction will inform the reader of the reason for writing the report. If the reason originated from a problem, the problem will be briefly mentioned here too.

The limitations of the report will be mentioned again in the introduction; that is, areas the report does and does not cover. In the introduction will also be mentioned the sources used and the way the data was collected, as well as a brief preview of the main ideas, and a precis of the present findings.

2. Problem

In this section, the problem is isolated and stated.

3. Past Findings

In this section, the writer will mention second-hand sources of past findings — what has been written before on the problem or on the subject in general, and the findings concluded from it.

4. Method

The research method used in the present study (i.e., yours) is stated here.

5. Present Findings

This section will be the body of your report, contained under headings and subheadings. In this section you will simply present your research, using your visual aids for further explanation and clarification if necessary. Use the passive voice (for example, "it was found") and write objectively (avoid mentioning your opinion and/or feelings). As mentioned above, you need to present your information clearly and logically, thinking of time and/or space order, or arranging your information and data otherwise, using either the direct or indirect method.

6. Discussion

Here you will discuss your research and what you have found. Again, use the passive voice and be objective. Present the discussion clearly and logically, thinking of the best order for clear reading and understanding. Sometimes the sections "Present Findings" and "Discussion" may be combined. Do whatever makes your own individual report easier to read and understand.

7. Conclusion

The final part of your report will be either a conclusion or a summary.

A conclusion is given at the end of a report in which the findings have been analysed, perhaps with stimulating questions for the reader. The conclusion revises the main findings of the report and answer any questions asked before the undertaking of the research.

A summary is simply a precis of the total report, outlining the main ideas. In general, summaries are written following reports which simply give information to the reader.

You will remember suggestion reports from the chapter on informal reports.

Formal reports may also be suggestion reports and the conclusion of a formal suggestion report will be the recommendation, or suggestion, of specific action to be taken.

After the End of the Report

When the report has been written, the bibliography will have to be compiled. This is the list, in alphabetical order, of all the texts which you have used for the second-hand information in your report, giving the titles, authors and publishers of each.

You may also have an appendix (or appendices) to include, depending on what kind of report it is. An appendix is simply any additional information which is not covered in the bibliography or in the report itself. For example, if you used a questionnaire to collect some or all of your data, then a copy of the questionnaire may be included in the appendix.

Analysis of a Simple Report

We are now going to look at an example of a formal report, page by page. This is an imaginary report on childhood obesity among Hong Kong schoolchildren. It is a very short, simplified report, but all the features of formal reports mentioned above are included. This is a fictitious example and all information quoted is therefore erroneous. However it will give you an idea of how a report should be presented, both in its layout, and language used. Here is the title fly page:

✍️

THE STUDY OF OBESITY IN HONG KONG SCHOOLCHILDREN
AGED 5–16

FROM 1988 TO 1998

The title page for this report would be as follows:

✍️

THE STUDY OF OBESITY IN HONG KONG SCHOOLCHILDREN
AGED 5–16

FROM 1988 TO 1998

Prepared for the Hong Kong Health Authority
Hong Kong

Prepared by:
Justin Lo
Rita Kwok
Susanna Wong
Nutrition in Hong Kong Children
Hong Kong University
19th December 1998

This is the usual format for the title page. Remember that the report may be bound on the left. If it is to be bound, move these title page sections a quarter of an inch to the right. There is no need to put a page number on the title page.

The next page should feature the "Terms of Reference." This gives the subject of the report and tells who it is for. It gives a very brief preview of the topic and the conclusions, if any. At the end of this section, the writer generally gives thanks, if appropriate, and invites further communication regarding the conclusions of the report. Here is what our "Terms of Reference" would look like:

Hong Kong University
Department of Nutrition and Dietetics

19th December 1998

Hong Kong Health Authority
119–121 Ashbourne Road
Wan Chai
Hong Kong

Dear Sir or Madam,

The following report, requested by the Hong Kong Health Authority, shows the increase in obesity in Hong Kong children between the ages of 5 and 16 years, in a ten-year study conducted between 1988 and 1998. We are sure that the results of our study will be of significant use to you, in particular our prediction of the likely future trends of obesity among Hong Kong children.

Our study of our sample over the ten years was aimed at examining:

1. changes in dietary habits,
2. changes in exercise habits, and
3. changes in cholesterol levels.

First-hand research involved interviewing 40 children per year, selected at random, in each of 80 Hong Kong government schools, i.e., 3,200 children interviewed per year, a total of 32,000 children over the ten years of our study. Second-hand research comes from the 1990 Hong Kong paper by John Wang, "Fat Is a Childhood Issue." Unfortunately childhood obesity has been very little researched in Hong Kong. We believe that our report is the most comprehensive to date.

Our research found that childhood obesity among Hong Kong schoolchildren has risen by 650% over the ten years of the study.

We thank you very much for asking us to compile this report for you, which has also constituted a relevant part of our doctorship. We would be extremely pleased to be able to discuss the results of our findings with you in person. Please do not hesitate to contact us at any time.

Yours sincerely,

Justin Lo
Rita Kwok
Suzanna Wong

The following page gives the Table of Contents. Use capital letters for main titles and lower case for subsections. Here the Table of Contents for our report:

✍🏻

TABLE OF CONTENTS

The next page begins the report itself. The title of the work goes at the top. The introduction follows, where the reader is given the reason for the writing of the report, and the problem, if any, is identified. The limitations of the report are given in the introduction. It is also useful to provide some details of the background to the report, if possible. Sources will be mentioned, as well as a brief preview of the work and its conclusions.

THE STUDY OF OBESITY IN HONG KONG SCHOOLCHILDREN
AGED 5–16

FROM 1988 TO 1998

INTRODUCTION

This report has been requested by the Hong Kong Health Authority following casual observation that obesity among Hong Kong schoolchildren would appear to be increasing. It spans ten years and covers 32,000 randomly sampled schoolchildren interviewed in 80 Hong Kong government schools. This research was limited to indigenous ethnic Chinese children only.

Sources used were the interviewing of all individuals represented in the sample and the 1990 Hong Kong paper entitled "Fat Is a Childhood Issue" by John Wang.

Data was collected through interviews, and the weighing, measuring and blood-testing of every child. We found a significant increase in childhood obesity among Hong Kong schoolchildren over the period of our research.

PROBLEM

This study was carried out in order to establish the percentage increase, if any, of obesity in Hong Kong schoolchildren aged 5–16 over a period of 10 years (1988–1998).

PAST FINDINGS

Unfortunately, the only past work done on the subject of childhood obesity is the 1990 paper by John Wang, entitled "Fat Is a Childhood Issue." Wang conducted research over a 4-year period (1986–1990) and cited an 141% increase in the number of obese children in Hong Kong over these years.

METHOD

Eighty government schools in a fair scattering of all geographic locations across Hong Kong were selected for this research. Each year, over a period of ten years, 40 randomly selected indigenous Hong Kong Chinese children from each school were interviewed, weighed and measured and underwent a blood test to establish blood cholesterol levels. The interview was conducted using the questionnaire presented in the Appendix. Answers to the questions were written by the researchers, following the children's spoken words.

PRESENT FINDINGS
Changes in Dietary Habits

The children interviewed were asked to keep a record of everything they ate in three one-week periods throughout the year. From analysis of the results of the children's records, significant conclusions could be drawn regarding the eating habits of Hong Kong schoolchildren over the ten-year period of study.

Changes in Exercise Habits

The children interviewed were asked to keep a record of their physical activities in three one-week periods throughout the year. From analysis of the results of these records, significant conclusions could be drawn regarding the exercise habits of the sample over the ten-year period of study.

Changes in Cholesterol Levels

Every child taking part in the research was medically blood-tested once at the end of each year for his or her level of cholesterol. From these medical results, significant conclusions could be drawn regarding the cholesterol levels of the sample over the 10-year period.

DISCUSSION

Diet

From 1988 to 1998, it was found that children's eating habits have changed significantly. Traditional Chinese fare of rice, meat and vegetables has largely been replaced by fast foods which are high in saturated fats. The growth of several well-known chains of fast-food restaurants in Hong Kong is one reason for this. It was found that children in secondary schools regularly if not daily snack and lunch in such outlets during the school week.

Primary schoolchildren are less likely to eat in fast-food restaurants while at school, but, of the overweight primary children interviewed, it was found that food high in saturated fats is regularly served at home. The research found that there is a significant level of parental concern that children should be "well fed"; the image of a thin child is still unacceptable to many Chinese parents.

The term "obese" was taken to mean weighing 20% or more of the ideal body weight as laid down by the standard of the Hong Kong Health Authority height and weight charts (Sze, 1965). As can be seen from the graph below, the numbers of children falling into the "obese" category rise across the ten years of the study.

(graph here)(1)

Exercise

The research found, over the ten years of the study, that levels of exercise had fallen significantly across the age range. It was found that this is because children are increasingly more house-bound. Parents, concerned about school grades, make children stay at home to study when they are not at school. A significant number of respondents cited that they were not allowed out to play because parents were concerned that something would happen to them. In addition to this, with the advent of home computers, a large representation of the sample spent their free time playing computer games instead of exercising.

Cholesterol

It was consistently found, over the ten years of the study, that cholesterol levels had risen among our sample. This was found to be due to the dietary changes mentioned above.

CONCLUSION

It can be concluded from our study that obesity has risen by 650% among Hong Kong schoolchildren. This can be regarded as a statistically significant increase. (2)

BIBLIOGRAPHY

Wang, J. "Fat Is a Childhood Issue." Hong Kong: Open University Press, 1990.

APPENDIX

Questionnaire used on sample of 32,000 Hong Kong schoolchildren from 1988–1998.

1. What is your favourite food?
2. How often do you eat it?
3. Why do you like it?
4. What do you usually eat at mealtimes at home?
5. How often do you eat these dishes?
6. Do adults at home encourage you to finish your food?
7. Do adults at home encourage you to eat more?
8. Do you eat snacks at school?
9. If so, does the snack come from home or do you buy it?
10. If your snack comes from home, who decides what it will be?
11. What do you usually eat for snack?
12. What do you usually eat for lunch?
13. Does your lunch come from home, or do you buy it?
14. At weekends, do you eat different dishes from what you eat during the week? If so, how are they different?
15. How do you get to school?
16. How do you get home from school?
17. Do you enjoy P.E. at school? Why/why not?

18. How do you spend your breaktimes?
19. How do you spend your lunchtimes?
20. Do you enjoy sports? If so, which one(s)? How often do you play?
21. Do you belong to a sports club or organization?
22. If you do not enjoy sports, why not?
23. After school or at weekends, do you play outside? If so, what do you play? How long do you play? If not, why not?
24. Do you think the amount of exercise you get is (a) not enough, (b) just right, or (c) too much?

Note that: (1) You will see that the graph is positioned close to the part of the report where it is first mentioned; and (2) a conclusion is given at the end, as the results have been analysed. There is no need to put the conclusion(s) on a new page.

Exercise I

Answer the following questions:
1. How does a formal report differ from an informal report?
2. Are formal reports used much in business?
3. When are formal reports used?
4. What should you write down before you start to write your report?
5. Are formal reports usually written using the direct or the indirect writing style?
6. When would you use the indirect method to write a formal report?
7. What are the two kinds of sources used when writing a formal report?
8. Give an example of each kind of source.
9. What is the best source of second-hand data?
10. What two kinds of order are important in a report?
11. Why are charts, tables and graphs important in the presentation of data?
12. Name four items included in the introduction.

13. What is the difference between a summary and a conclusion in a report?
14. What is the purpose of the "Terms of Reference" page?
15. What must you not bring in to a report?
16. Why are reports written in the passive voice?

Exercise II

Using the situation to polish your communication skills, obtain an actual formal report, either from a company, or perhaps from a university or college. At home, read through it with a view to assessing it, based on what you have learned about the writing and presentation of formal reports. Using a pencil, write comments on it; be critical. Does it contain all the features of a formal report? How would you improve it? Remember to make positive comments if they are deserved (i.e., if (some of) the report is well-written/well presented)!

Bring the report you have assessed to the class and change it with that of another student at the end of the lesson. Take his or hers home, and read through his or her evaluation of the report he or she has obtained. Assess your partner's assessment of his or her report. Bring all reports to the next lesson to discuss in pairs, until mutual agreement is reached.

Task I

Divide into small groups of 3–4 students each. As a class, you are going to write a report, with each small group working on a different section of it. As a class, vote for the title among the following:

1. Report on the damage done to your company's offices after a minor fire, as requested by an insurance agent.

2. Report on the "climate" of Hong Kong from the hand-over to date, as requested by the Hong Kong Chamber of Commerce.

3. Report on the possibility of opening a new factory dealing with your products in the Philippines, as requested by the Philippines Consulate.

4. Report on the recent strike by all women in your company, demanding equal pay for equal work, as requested by the union.

5. Report on the attitude of the Hong Kong population towards the American President Bill Clinton, in view of the recent reports on his private life, as requested by a research company.

Invent all the information. Your aim is not for accuracy in the content, but for proper layout, the good use of the passive voice and clear, ordered, logical thought which shows throughout the report. Here are the different sections, each group is to choose a section and write it. Compile, as a group, a rough draft first, and discuss and alter it until there is common agreement on the final version. Each section should be no longer than 100 words.

• Purpose statement
• Introduction
• Problem (if any)
• Past findings
• Method
• Present findings
• Conclusion

Task II

Choose another partner. Pretend that you are both inspection officers from the "Department of Health and Hygiene." Your office has received several complaints about the hygiene standards in several noodle shops in the backstreets of Wan Chai. In pairs, source out a Wan Chai noodle shop and order food. Make detailed notes of the cleanliness of the premises, the servers, the bowls and cups, the people handing the money, and the food itself. Is there a no-smoking section? Are the staff smoking? Inspect the toilets, and, if you can, the kitchens. Make notes on the shop frontage. Are the pavement and gutter in front of the shop clean? Does pollution from vehicles enter the shop? Is there a smelly drain in the road? If possible, walk around to the back of the shop and make notes on the cleanliness you observe there.

At home, write a report on your observations, containing all the features of a formal report. As you are working in pairs, do half of the report each. Decide between yourselves who will do what. In class, work together to polish your report to its final version.

10

Minutes for Meetings

In this chapter, you will learn:
- what minutes are;
- why minutes for meetings are important;
- how to write good minutes for meetings.

Minutes are written records of the things said or decided at a meeting. It is important to record what happens in meetings for future reference. This is especially true for public companies, where the shareholders need to know what has happened in the meetings of the company they own.

Writing down everything that happens in a meeting is called "taking the minutes." The "minutes" are the detailed notes about the meeting. It is not necessary to write down everything that is said in a meeting; what is important is to note down the important things that are said which should lead to actions being taken. Tape-recording the meeting can be helpful.

To take the minutes well, you need good, clear, simple English. The minutes are written in the past tense in English, because they are about a meeting already finished.

There may be a reference number for the whole agenda of the meeting. This number is also used for the minutes, for example, Ref. ABC/21.10.97. The reference number has to be written at the top of the page.

To begin, you must write the name of the group of people that met, for example, "Board of Governors," or "Board of Directors," or "English Department Staff," or "Sales Staff." You must also write where and when they met.

Look at the example below.

✎

Ref. ABC/21.10.97

MINUTES OF THE MEETING OF SALES STAFF HELD IN THE CONFERENCE ROOM AT 10.00 A.M. ON TUESDAY, 21ST OCTOBER 1997

You will see that the example shows the people who met, where they met and when they met.

After writing who was at the meeting, when it happened and where it happened, you need to write the names of all the people who were at the meeting, and, if any of these people had a title, you must include it.

Writing the Minutes, Step by Step

Let us work with the example above. With the names of all the people who attended this sales meeting, look at the example now:

✎

Ref. ABC/21.10.97

MINUTES OF THE MEETING OF SALES STAFF HELD IN THE CONFERENCE ROOM AT 10.00 A.M. ON TUESDAY, 21ST OCTOBER 1997

PRESENT: Mr. A. B. CHAN, Director of Sales
		Ms. C. D. DENG, Senior Sales Manager
		Mr. F. FONG, Sales Manager
		Mr. G. H. LUI, Sales Representative
		Ms. I. HO, Sales Representative

Next, you should write another list of the names of anyone who should have attended the meeting but was absent for some reason. You should call this list "APOLOGIES FOR ABSENCE."

For example:

✍

APOLOGIES FOR ABSENCE: Ms. J. K. LIM, Sales Negotiator

During a meeting, one or more people may be present only for a part of the meeting. In this case, you should write the name of that person, and show which part of the meeting he or she attended.

Each separate topic of a meeting is called an "item." Look at the example below:

✍

PRESENT FOR ITEM 3: Mr. I. NO, Consultant

Next, write the name of the person writing the minutes, yourself! Call this "IN ATTENDANCE."

✍

IN ATTENDANCE: Mr. G. LING, Personal Assistant

The secretary of a meeting plays important roles to ensure the accuracy of the minutes of a meeting

The writing of the minutes begins by stating that the minutes from the last meeting have been read, approved, and signed. Copies of these minutes from the previous meeting are given to everybody who should have them. They may be read, approved and signed by the chairperson now.

There may be something from the last minutes which must be discussed at this meeting. You can show this with the title "MATTERS ARISING FROM LAST MEETING."

Here is an example. The words actually spoken are printed in italics. Your minutes on what was said are printed underneath.

Mr. Lui: *Ms. Ho and I, as you will remember, had received a quote from Acme Singapore on 1,000 pieces of our XYA range which we were considering. We have now accepted the quote but Acme has just now sent us an e-mail asking for our proposal for 10,000 pieces.*

Mr. Chan: *Have you responded to Acme's e-mail?*

Mr. Lui: *Not yet, it only came through this morning.*

Mr. Chan: *As it's not urgent, let's leave it until our next meeting. Are we all agreed on that?*

All: *Yes.*

MATTERS ARISING FROM THE LAST MEETING

XYA for Acme Singapore

Mr. Lui and Ms. Ho had received a quote from Acme Singapore on 1,000 pieces of our XYA range which they were considering. Mr. Lui and Ms. Ho have now accepted Acme's quote but Acme now wants a proposal on 10,000 pieces. It was agreed to defer the decision on this proposal until the next meeting.

Now you are ready to write the minutes of this meeting. To do this, you write the important things said by each person in the meeting, and note down all the decisions reached on each item on the agenda of the meeting. You should also write down all the decisions which have been put off to a later date, and also all the suggestions mentioned in the meeting which were rejected. This is given the title "NEW BUSINESS."

The person chairing the meeting should state very clearly what has been decided at the end of each item. Below, you will see the four main items in our imaginary sales meeting as they are actually spoken, and then underneath them, these same short conversations written as minutes. Again, in our examples, what was said in our imaginary meeting is printed in italics. The Minutes are printed underneath.

As mentioned before, you should always use the past tense when taking minutes, as you are reporting what was said.

- Mr. Lui proposed ...
- Ms. Ho seconded ...
- Mr. Chan commented ...
- Ms. Deng questioned ...
- Mr. Fong objected ...
- Ms. Ho disagreed ...
- Mr. Lui abstained ...
- Mr. Chan said ...
- Ms. Ho suggested ...

Each topic on the agenda is called an item. You should number the items as you write about what was said. Give each item a title. At the end of each item, you should note what decision was reached, and/or what action was taken. Using passive forms is best, where possible. For example:

- It was decided that ...
- It was agreed that ...
- The proposal was rejected ...
- The decision was deferred ...
- The meeting was postponed ...
- The matter was resolved ...
- The proposal was received ...

Our sales meeting example had four items to cover. Here they are, first, as they are spoken, and underneath, as they are in minutes form as taken by Personal Assistant Mr. G. Ling.

The meeting begins:

Mr. Chan: *Good morning everyone. Okay, let's begin with item 1 on our agenda this morning. Ms. Ho, I believe you have some news on Good Company, Malaysia?*

Ms. Ho: *Yes, I propose a quote of 560,000 Hong Kong dollars to Good Company for 80,000 pieces of our RM/HKG.*

Mr. Chan: *Yes, that seems a fair quote. Do we have any objections? (Silence.) Okay. 560,000 dollars approved for Good Company.*

You write the minute:

Item 1. QUOTE FOR GOOD COMPANY, MALAYSIA

Ms. Ho proposed a quote of HK$560,000 to Good Company, Malaysia for 80,000 pieces of our RM/HKG. The proposal was agreed.

The meeting continues:

Ms. Deng: *Okay, Item 2. We are still having problems with our GTY iron components for Super Company, Japan: the specification is not compatible with their iron.*

Mr. Chan: *Yes. I suggest a visit to Super Company with Ms. Deng in the coming week. It might be a good idea for Mr. Lui to go too. Our engineers are both in Shenzhen but we need to bring them out as well.*

Mr. Lui: *Do you think such a trip would be necessary at this point? I propose that Ms. Ho and I try to clear up the problem with the engineers from here first, as we have only just received this complaint from Super Company.*

Mr. Chan: *No, I think we should make the trip. Super Company is a new and potentially very big customer which we don't want to lose. Are we all agreed?*

All: *Yes.*

Mr. Chan: *Okay. I confirm the approval of a trip to Japan in the coming week. Myself, Ms. Deng, Mr. Lui and the engineers will go.*

You write the minute:

✎

Item 2. GTY PROBLEM AT SUPER COMPANY, JAPAN

Super Company, Japan is still not happy with the specification of the GTY iron components. Mr. Chan suggested a visit to Super Company with Ms. Deng and Mr. Lui and with the engineers in the coming week. Mr. Lui objected to the suggestion and proposed further communication between Super Company and himself and Ms. Ho first. Mr. Lui's objection was overruled and the visit was approved.

Consultant Mr. I. No, from Know-all Consultants, is now introduced into the conference room for Item 3. The meeting continues:

Mr. Chan: *Ah, Mr. No! Good morning.*

Mr. No: *Good morning everyone.*

Mr. Chan: *Mr. No is with us for Item 3 this morning. Perhaps you would like to share with us, Mr. No, your ideas for the 8XXD line.*

Mr. No: *Yes. From what Mr. Chan has told me, your 8XXD range is very unprofitable. I propose that you scrap this line completely, and retrench the four members of staff working on this line. I would also advise that you recruit a Sales Manager with a specialization in PCB to assist Ms. Deng with the JJ482 range.*

Ms. Deng: *Yes, I think these suggestions are just what we need.*

Mr. Fong: *I agree. The 8XXD line should definitely go.*

Mr. Chan: *Yes, excellent recommendations. Do we all accept and approve Mr. No's proposals?*

All: *Yes.*

Mr. Chan: *Good. Thank you, Mr. No, for your suggestions.*

Mr. No: *My pleasure. I have left my full written report with your secretary.*

Mr. Chan: *Thank you. Goodbye.*

Mr. No: *Goodbye.*

You write the minute:

Item 3. PROPOSAL BY MR. I. NO, KNOW-ALL CONSULTANTS

Mr. I. No from Know-all Consultants was present for this item. Mr. No proposed that we scrap the 8XXD line and retrench the four members of staff working on this line. He also suggested recruiting a Sales Manager to assist Ms. Deng with the JJ482 range. Both proposals by Mr. No were approved and accepted.

The meeting continues:

Mr. Chan: *Right, now we come to the final item on the agenda. Ms. Ho, could you please give us the Sales Programme for the YUU fuse wire?*

Ms. Ho: *Yes, certainly. (Ms. Ho stands and gives her presentation on the whiteboard. Those present in the meeting review the programme.)*

Mr. Chan: *Good. Do we give final approval for the YUU Sales Programme?*

All: *Yes.*

Mr. Chan: *Excellent.*

You write the minute:

Item 4. SALES PROGRAMME FOR YUU FUSE WIRE

Ms. Ho presented the Company's proposed Sales Programme for the YUU fuse wire. The programme was reviewed and given final approval.

The final item on an agenda for a meeting is "ANY OTHER BUSINESS." This means any item that anyone present in the meeting feels important to discuss but which has not been officially listed on the agenda. If you have to write the minute "ANY OTHER BUSINESS," write it as you would write any other item on the official agenda.

In our imaginary sales meeting, Mr. Chan continues by asking if there is "any other business." See below:

Mr. Chan: *Do we have any other business?*

Ms. Deng: *Yes. I was wondering if it may be worth considering looking around now for office premises in China, in line with our projected expansion.*

Mr. Chan: *I agree, but the renting of a second office now is not within this year's annual budget. Do we agree to defer this decision until the beginning of the next fiscal year?*

All: *Yes.*

Mr. Chan: *Good.*

You write the minute:

ANY OTHER BUSINESS

Second Office in China

Ms. Deng mentioned that it may be worthwhile to consider starting to look around now for a premises suitable as a second office in China. Mr. Chan rejected this suggestion, saying that the renting of a second office was not within the annual budget. It was agreed to defer the decision until the beginning of the next fiscal year.

Finally, the date and place of the next meeting is mentioned. In our example, the date of the next meeting has been postponed. Look at what Mr. Chan says as he brings the meeting to a close:

Mr. Chan: *Well, everything on the agenda has been covered this morning. Our next meeting?*

Mr. Lui: *It will have to be on the 4th of November, due to your trip to Japan.*

Mr. Chan: *4th of November? Okay, in two weeks from today. 10 o'clock, here in the conference room.*

(All members of the Sales Meeting leave)

You write the minute:

DATE AND PLACE OF NEXT MEETING

The meeting of sales staff scheduled at 10.00 a.m. on Tuesday, 28th October 1997, has been postponed due to the business trip of Mr. Chan and Ms. Deng to Japan on 27th October. It was agreed that the next sales meeting would take place at 10.00 a.m. in the conference room on 4th Tuesday November.

Finally, you have to write the time at which the meeting ended. You can simply write, "MEETING ADJOURNED AT 12.05 P.M.,

TUESDAY, 21ST OCTOBER 1997." You should sign your name under this, with your title in the company.

Your minutes have now finished. You, as the writer of the minutes, should type the minutes up neatly no later than 24 hours after writing them. The chairperson of the meeting will sign and date these minutes at the beginning of the next meeting, to show that they are correct.

Here then are the minutes of our sales meeting in full:

✍

Ref. ABC/21.10.97

MINUTES OF THE MEETING OF SALES STAFF HELD IN THE CONFERENCE ROOM AT 10:00 A.M. ON TUESDAY, 21ST OCTOBER 1997

PRESENT: Mr. A. B. CHAN, Director of Sales
Ms. C. D. DENG, Senior Sales Manager
Mr. F. FONG, Sales Manager
Mr. G. H. LUI, Sales Representative
Ms. I. HO, Sales Representative

APOLOGIES FOR ABSENCE: Ms. J. K. LIM, Sales Negotiator

PRESENT FOR ITEM 3: Mr. I. NO, Consultant

IN ATTENDANCE: Mr. G. LING, Personal Assistant

MATTERS ARISING FROM THE LAST MEETING

XYA for Acme Singapore

Mr. Lui and Ms. Ho had received a quote from Acme Singapore on 1,000 pieces of our XYA range which they were considering. Mr. Lui and Ms. Ho have now accepted Acme's quote but Acme now wants a proposal on 10,000 pieces. It was agreed to defer the decision on this proposal until the next meeting.

NEW BUSINESS

Item 1. QUOTE FOR GOOD COMPANY, MALAYSIA

Ms. Ho proposed a quote of HK$560,000 to Good Company, Malaysia for 80,000 pieces of our RM/HKG. The proposal was agreed.

Item 2. GTY PROBLEM AT SUPER COMPANY, JAPAN

Super Company, Japan is still not happy with the specification of the GTY iron components. Mr. Chan suggested a visit to Super Company with Ms. Deng and Mr. Lui and with the engineers in the coming week. Mr. Lui objected to the suggestion and proposed further communication between Super Company and himself and Ms. Ho first. Mr. Lui's objection was overruled and the visit was approved.

Item 3. PROPOSAL BY MR. I. NO, KNOW-ALL CONSULTANTS

Mr. I. No from Know-all Consultants was present for this item. Mr. No proposed that we scrap the 8XXD line and retrench the four members of staff working on this line. He also suggested recruiting a Sales Manager to assist Ms. Deng with the JJ482 range. Both proposals by Mr. No were approved and accepted.

Item 4. SALES PROGRAMME FOR YUU FUSE WIRE

Ms. Ho presented the Company's proposed Sales Programme for the YUU fuse wire. The programme was reviewed and given final approval.

ANY OTHER BUSINESS

Second Office in China

Ms. Deng mentioned that it may be worthwhile to consider starting to look around now for a premises suitable as a second office in China. Mr. Chan rejected this suggestion, saying that the renting of a second office was not within the annual budget. It was agreed to defer the decision until the beginning of the next fiscal year.

DATE AND PLACE OF NEXT MEETING

The meeting of sales staff scheduled at 10.00 a.m. on Tuesday, 28th October 1997, has been postponed due to the business trip of Mr. Chan and Ms. Deng to Japan on 27th October. It was agreed that the next sales meeting would take place at 10.00 a.m. in the conference room on 4th Tuesday November.

MEETING ADJOURNED AT 12.05 P.M., TUESDAY, 21ST OCTOBER 1997.

G. LING, Personal Assistant, 22ND OCTOBER 1997

This chapter has taught you the following:

1. Minutes are the record of important things said, and decisions made in meetings.
2. The minutes follow the agenda closely, item by item.
3. Minutes must be written in clear, simple English.
4. Correct past tenses are very important.

Exercise

The following ten sentences are badly worded minutes. Rewrite the minutes in better English using the terms below the sentences:

1. Mr. Wong said it was okay to ship on the 24th.
2. Ms. Kwok said she didn't like the proposal.
3. Mr. Lui said it might be a good idea to give a lower quote.
4. Mrs. Tu said she thought it would be better to make the decision later.
5. Ms. Luk said she really didn't want to recruit another secretary.
6. Mr. Choi thought it might be a better idea to lay off two sales staff.
7. All the people in the meeting said they agreed with the proposal.
8. All the people in the meeting said they thought the proposal was good.
9. All the people in the meeting didn't want to consider the suggestion.
10. Everybody left at 10.06 a.m.

- was agreed
- suggested
- was approved
- agreed
- disagreed
- was rejected

- proposed
- was adjourned
- was not in favour of

REMEMBER! In English two phrases commonly used in minutes take the infinitive followed by the gerund:

- to propose do*ing* something
- to suggest do*ing* something

Task I

You are the Managing Director of a manufacturing company. Over the past 12 months, you see that the company does not need so many design engineers, because your company has reduced its product lines. There are four design engineers in the company, but two of them must go.

You meet with two of your top managers to decide on which two design engineers to retrench and which two to keep.

Divide into equal groups of three. Together, decide on and write the dialogue for this meeting, using the information about the four engineers, given below. Keep the English short and simple. Keep the meeting fairly short!

1. Mr. Chung
    Age: 26
    Education: university degree in design engineering
    Experience: two years with the company after leaving university
    Marital status: to be married soon
    Personality: very friendly, sociable

Work: first class
Other information: eager to climb to the top.

2. Mr. Lee
    Age: 55
    Education: F5 graduate; self-trained from apprenticeship with
    the company
    Experience: 38 years with the company
    Marital status: married with four children, two at university in
    the United States
    Personality: friendly, quiet
    Work: slow but steady; reliable
    Other information: due to retire in 5 years

3. Mr. So
    Age: 37
    Education: F5 then tutorial college, diploma in engineering;
    learned through experience
    Experience: 18 years with the company
    Marital status: married, two young children
    Personality: prefers to work alone, not sociable
    Work: excellent
    Other information: just bought a flat with heavy mortgage
    commitments

4. Mr. Cheuk
    Age: 31
    Education: Engineering Degree, Swiss M.B.A.
    Experience: one year with the company
    Marital status: single
    Personality: unpleasant, bossy, does not like dealing with
    people
    Work: refuses to work overtime; careless, not a hard worker
    Other information: the nephew of one of the directors in the
    company; worked as a funds manager
    before joining the company

Task II

When you have finished, exchange your meeting dialogue with that of another group. With this new dialogue, work together on writing the minutes for it. Call it "Item 1. THE RETRENCHING OF TWO DESIGN ENGINEERS." When finished, return the minutes to the group who wrote the dialogue. Check your papers to see if the minutes written by the other group are correct.

Task III

Here is what was said in a meeting of the Board of Directors of a bus company, "Crazy Bus Company." Write the minutes for this meeting. Give each speaker a name and a title as a member of the Board. Here is the meeting as it was spoken:

A: Yes, we had decided to come to some agreement today on whether or not to allow drunks on our buses. Do we have any comments?

B: Of course we can't allow drunks! They are noisy and smelly and frighten the other passengers.

C: I agree. But the problem is, how do we know how drunk someone is?

D: Well, how about just not allowing extremely drunken people on the buses? I mean, if they are too drunk to climb on?

B: Yes, I agree! How about instructing our drivers to drive off at full speed if a drunk tries to get onto a bus?

A: Excellent idea! What do the rest of you think about that?

All: Yes, we all agree!

A: Good! Let's now get on to Item 1: to consider painting all our buses fluorescent orange.

E: Well, I think it's a good idea. The other bus companies have their buses painted in dull colours. If we paint all our buses bright orange, our buses will be very visible.

C: Yes. Passengers will be able to see our buses coming from a very long way off.

B: But is this a good thing? As you know, we are still trying to get passengers to use our buses more than any other buses. If they can see our buses coming from a long way off, they may move to another bus stop. If we keep our buses painted like the others, by the time passengers realize it's one of ours, it'll be too late for them to move and they'll be forced to take our bus.

A: Hmmm. A good point.

D: Yes, I agree with B. I think that more passengers will be forced to ride our buses if we keep our buses looking like all the other buses, for the reasons that B gave.

A: Hmmm. Yes, this is a very good point. In fact I have changed my mind about the orange and I agree with B. What about the rest of you?

All: Yes, okay. Whatever gets the passengers on our buses is top priority.

A: Okay, let's stick with the same colours. Now let's move on to Item 2. To consider taking all the seats out of our entire bus fleet. Any opinions?

B: I absolutely agree. That way, we can cram as many passengers as possible into our buses, upstairs and down.

C: Yes, I like the idea. Who needs to sit down? Hong Kong is small, journey times are short. During rush hours especially, it is very difficult to get a seat on any bus. Hong Kong people are used to standing and shouldn't mind having no chance to sit.

D: What about old people, pregnant ladies and the handicapped?

E: Yes, this might be a problem. But the percentage of pas-
     sengers in these categories is very small. Many old people and
     even some pregnant women will not mind standing. If they
     really want to sit down, they can take another company's bus.

A: Are we all agreed then?

All: Yes.

A: Right, Item 3. To consider employing ex-racing car drivers
     for our entire fleet.

E: Yes, it's time we did this. We have very serious competition
     here from the other bus companies in Hong Kong. To put it
     simply, we are just not fast enough. I know for a fact that our
     most serious competitor, Deathwish Buses, has hired eight of
     Macau's top ex-racing champions.

F: Yes, and they can get from Happy Valley to Kennedy Town
     in under 8 minutes, all stops included, and this in the rush
     hour.

A: Well, if this is the case, we are behind the times. Hong Kong
     is a fast-moving city, and our buses must be fast too. As they
     say, time is money, and if we can save passengers time by
     faster speeds than Deathwish Buses, it will be a good thing for
     the company.

B: Yes! Everybody will want to ride our buses!

All: Yes, I agree!

A: Excellent! C, will you start the advertising process for ex-
     racing car drivers? Remember, we want the fastest.

C: My pleasure.

A: Good. Now, Item 4. To consider a pay rise for bus drivers —
     how much should we be looking at?

F: Well, since we are going to be employing the fastest drivers in
     Hong Kong, I would say that an attractive salary would be a
     top priority in order to recruit them.

B: Yes, absolutely. How about 400% up from the present rate?

C: Yes, it seems a good suggestion.

A: Does anyone want to add to that? (Silence). Right then, a 400% increase over the present rate it is. Are we all agreed? All approve?

All: Yes.

A: Excellent. Do we have any other business?

E: Well, I suggest raising bus fares to meet the higher costs of employing these new drivers.

A: Good idea.

E: How about a matching increase? 400% on the fares?

F: Yes, that seems sensible.

A: Does anyone object to a 400% increase in fares?

All: No.

A: Good. Passengers should not mind the increase given that they will be getting the fastest ride in town and so be saving time. Do we all approve E's suggestion?

All: Yes.

A: Okay then, that ends today's meeting. Our next meeting?

B: Next week, same place, same time.

A: Good, until next week, then. (All leave).

11

Employment Communication

In this chapter, you will learn:
- how to write résumé and application letter professionally;
- how to prepare for job interviews.

When you apply for your first job, being able to communicate well enough to sell yourself to your future employer is very important. As you move through your career, you will find that you will change your job position, sometimes frequently, as is often the case in Hong Kong. Again, with job changes, you will need to be able to communicate your skills and potential to new employers, in the hope that they will employ you.

You will need to know how to organize and present your résumé or curriculum vitae (C.V.), a letter of application, and perhaps a follow-up letter. These are the written communication skills. At an interview, you will also need to know how to sell yourself well in a verbal situation as you talk with the interviewer. Finally, your body language says a lot about you. You need to be aware of the non-verbal communication which your body is giving, and use it to your advantage.

Your First Job

Before you apply for your first job, you will need to do some serious thinking about what kind of career is best for you. You can ask a

Vocational Counsellor to help you through this process, but this will be expensive. By asking yourself six basic questions, you should be able to see a clearer picture of where your job path lies.

1. What is my level of education?
2. What salary do I need?
3. What working conditions would I prefer?
4. Where (in Hong Kong or in the world) would I prefer to work?
5. What field of work do I want to be in?
6. How important is it for me to climb to the top of what I want to do?

Think about the answers to these questions. However, it may be possible that you do not have very clear career ideas or goals. If this is the case, you still have to plan ahead, to think about the choices open to you that would give you maximum satisfaction.

The following questions may help you to choose a career path:

1. What are my capabilities?
2. What skills have I learned and how can I show that I have these skills?
3. What am I best at doing?
4. Doing what makes me happiest? Does there exist a job title which involves this?
5. If not, can I create a job for myself?
6. Could I start my own business doing what makes me happiest?
7. Am I good at organizing people or am I happier in a team? Happiest working alone?
8. How are my communication skills? Can I communicate in another language?

The answers to all of these questions are useful if you are applying for your first job, but also of course if you decide on a change of career if you are not happy with what you are doing now.

Collect Information

If you are still at college or university, you can find information on the career you are considering:

- in your library,
- at your career advice centre,
- by taking a summer job or sandwich course in your field,
- by interviewing someone who is doing what you would like to do,
- by joining any societies related to the career you are considering.

Looking Through the Job Market

Finding a job that you are happy with will mean a lot of work for you! The most well-known place to look is the classified job advertisements in the local newspapers. But they are not the only source. If you can network — tell everybody you know that you are looking for a certain kind of job, or ask who they know who might be interested in you — you can sometimes be lucky enough to find the kind of job you are looking for. Another idea is to write to companies for whom you would like to work, asking if they have any openings, and enclosing your résumé. This is called prospecting for a job. If you are a student, your lecturers may have contacts in the field you are considering.

Selling Yourself — Your Résumé

Getting a job means selling yourself. It is possible to obtain the job of your dreams by directly communicating with the employer, by phone or in person, and getting a positive response by making a very good first impression. In fact this is the most favourable approach, as it gives the employer a chance to "see what he or she would get," and gives you a chance to "show him or her what you've got," without the first step of sending off your résumé and covering letter, which, in most cases, do not give you as good a chance of getting the job. Approaching an employer directly, however, is yet another skill to be learned and is not relevant to this chapter. Therefore, you will have to know how to put together your résumé to present to an employer as a first step, in place of yourself.

Your résumé is the package you send to employers to sell your services. Admittedly, it is not the best way to let employers get a good

The key idea of sending in application is to get a reply

feeling about you, so you have to write your résumé in such a way that you seem to the employer to be good enough to interview, better, even, than the other applicants.

The job market in Hong Kong is extremely competitive. Your application may be one of hundreds which land on the desk of the employer. On paper, your qualifications may be just as good as those of the next applicant. How do you give yourself the very best possible chance of getting the job you want in the face of such heavy competition? The applicants most interesting to an employer will be those who seem on paper to be the best out of all the people who applied. The first step is to make your paperwork make you seem the best.

What is "the best"? The best kind of application clearly tells the employer how he or she and the company would benefit by employing you.

It is extremely important to write a résumé which stands out from the rest. A well-written résumé does not just simply list your qualifications, it is one of the most important tools you have to sell yourself. The whole aim of the résumé is to get you to the interview. An employer can take 30 seconds to briefly read through a résumé. Any which are poorly presented, difficult to read, or whose qualifications are irrelevant to the job offered, will be immediately rejected. Your résumé should not be a begging letter to an employer whom you humbly hope will ask you for an interview. You need to control your written application so that the information you present to your employer will make him think that, out of all the applicants, you are the one who will be of the greatest benefit to his company.

Which Résumé Style?

Your résumé must show that you can organize information and present it in a clear, concise way. There are two main styles to choose from:

- Chronological
- Functional

The Chronological Résumé

This is the style of résumé which is preferred by corporate executive employers. It gives information about you starting from the present time and going backwards in time. Both your work experience and educational qualifications are shown in the reverse order which gives employers the best idea of a person's career path, their past achievements and qualifications. This style is best if you have a lot of experience in your chosen field and can show that you are moving ahead in your career. Here is an example of a chronological résumé.

WONG Kam Wah James

Address: Flat A, 19/F, Victory Court
        888 Poon Wah Street
        Kowloon
        Hong Kong
Tel. 23456789 (Office)

Tel. 29876543 (Home)
Fax. 20987654 (Home)
Mobile 99900999
Pager 71111111 a/c 111

WORK EXPERIENCE

July 1993–Present	Senior Sales Manager for SuperAce Company, Hung Hom, Hong Kong.

- Managed a team of 6 Sales Executives responsible for the ABC product line and its sales throughout the Asia-Pacific region.
- Turned around the declining sales figures of 1993 to achieve a 72% growth.
- Initiated and exceed a target of US$3 million of sales in the last fiscal year (1995–1996).
- Was solely responsible for the development of present sales training programme.
- Provide continuous support and on-the-job training to executive team in all areas.

May 1991– June 1993	Sales Manager for GreatCo., Kowloon Bay, Hong Kong.

- Was responsible for sales of GoodPro CDE range over South-East Asia.
- Managed a sales team of 3 Sales Engineers covering 12 distribution channels.
- Reached projected sales target of US$2 million, exceeded in years 1992 and 1993.
- Expanded customer base over South-East Asia, including a start in Japan.
- Increased the number of accounts from 14 to 25 in Hong Kong.

January 1989– April 1991	Sales Executive, Fantastico, Wan Chai, Hong Kong.

- Consistently achieved sales targets on HIJ line for two consecutive years (1990 and 1991).
- Assisted senior management in developing advertising and promotional programmes.
- Trained new employees in product lines.
- Collected market intelligence and trend information of the China and Hong Kong market segments.

EDUCATION

September– December 1988	London School of Economics, England. P.G.C. (Distinction), Sales and Marketing, Intensive Study.
September 1985– June 1988	University of London, England. B.A. (Hons.) Business Management

SKILLS AND ABILITIES

Proficient in Word Perfect, Windows, Excel etc.

Recognized exceptional people skills

PERSONAL ACHIEVEMENTS

Business Management Student of the Year (1987–1988)

LANGUAGES

Cantonese (fluent)

English (good)

Putonghua (good)

French (working knowledge)

RELEVANT INFORMATION

Will relocate and/or travel.

INTERESTS

Chess, heliskiing, tennis, theatre.

REFERENCES

Upon request.

The Functional Résumé

The functional résumé pays attention to a person's qualifications and abilities rather than on his or her past work record. It is a possible style to use if you have recently graduated and have little or no employment experience.

In Hong Kong, people may change jobs frequently, and this may be a better style to use if this is the case for you. The functional style of résumé would also be better if you have not worked continuously over a period of time, or have worked in several different kinds of jobs which have all needed the same kinds of skills from you.

However, employers generally do not like this style of résumé. They feel that it may be hiding the fact that a person has changed jobs many times over a short period, or that there are big spaces between jobs which cannot be explained. To repeat, it is the best style to use for students who have just graduated or are just about to graduate.

Really the only time an employer would be happy with a functional résumé is if you are changing careers, because this type of résumé shows the employer where your talents or strengths lie. Here is an example of a functional résumé, that of a student recently graduated. Achievements are usually written in backward order of importance for the job in question.

✍

LEE Tak Cheung Jason

Address: Flat D, 8/F, Battle Court
           444 Hin Yick Street
           Kowloon
           Hong Kong

Tel. 23232323 (Office)
Tel. 29292929 (Home)
Fax. 23232324 (Home)
Mobile 91111119
Pager 76543210 a/c 999

MARKETING/SALES SKILLS
- Researched and organized a market research project as Project Coordinator for Hewtell Pachkard.
- Successfully conducted market research survey for Department of Health (Hong Kong) into dietary habits of office workers.
- Set up and ran sales analysis and planning for college library.
- Directly sold "Magical Diet" drink throughout Hong Kong — achieved a consistent personal quota turnover of HK$100,000 per month.

COMMUNICATION SKILLS
- Wrote two reports (63 pages and 84 pages) on the results and analysis of market survey projects for Hewtell Pachkard. Presented these reports to Business Development Manager.
- Prepared a written report for the Department of Health on the market research survey mentioned above.

- Gave a radio interview (Radio 888, Hong Kong) based on the results of the above market research.
- Co-wrote a column for publication in the *Hong Kong News* on the dietary habits of Hong Kong office workers.

MANAGEMENT SKILLS
- Supervised a team of 8 market researchers for the Department of Health.
- Acted as student representative in the successful negotiation of a minimum pay claim by students of summer job employers in the retail industry.
- Supervised a team of four Project Coordinators, Hewtell Pachkard market research.

EDUCATION
1994–1997   Hong Kong Polytechnic
                    B.A. (Hons) Business Studies.

EMPLOYMENT
1997 (summer employment)
Project Coordinator.
Initiated expansion on 1996 project of Hewtell Pachkard's XYZ product line in Japan.
1996 (summer employment)
Project Coordinator with Business Development Manager, Hewtell Pachkard, Hong Kong.
Was solely responsible for market research into niche in Japan for the XYZ product line.
1995 (summer employment)
Pioneered market research survey for Department of Health, Hong Kong.

SPECIAL SKILLS
Proficient in Windows 95, Excel.
Fluent in Putonghua

INTERESTS
Surfing, football, computers.

REFERENCES
Upon request.

Organizing Your Résumé

All résumés have similar parts, but organizing your résumé to your best advantage is important. A good résumé will clearly show that you have the qualifications and skills necessary for the job on offer. A good résumé will focus on this so that your weaknesses will not show.

All résumés should have a main heading, information on your education and qualifications, information on your work experience, information on your skills and abilities, information on any special awards or achievements, and information on your hobbies or interests.

The Heading

The heading for a résumé should be your name, address and contact numbers. Do not write the word "RÉSUMÉ," or "CURRICULUM VITAE" at the top! Give your full name, and the address where you normally receive letters. Give a telephone number where you can be reached during the day, with mobile, fax and pager numbers if you have them. It is important to be contactable, employers may call the next person on their shortlist which may mean a job lost for you.

Education

You should begin with your most advanced qualification, which may or may not be your most recent. You need to mention the name of the college(s) or university(ies) which you attended and its/their geographical location. After stating your most advanced qualification, list your other qualifications, going backwards from the most recent to the oldest. Mention subjects that you studied only if they are relevant to the job on offer. Mention the dates of your courses, or the month and year of graduation. If you have not yet completed your diploma or degree, mention when you expect to graduate with the title of your degree!

Work Experience

The most important part of your résumé is the section detailing your previous work record. If you have been in the workplace for some time and what you have done can contribute to the job advertised, put the section on your work experience before the section on your education and qualifications. Start with your most recent employment and work backwards, selecting all those areas of your work experience which are important for the job in question. Mention the name of the company and its location, dates of your employment there in months and years, your job titles, and the activities and duties you did which would be important for the job in question. Give details of your accomplishments, showing the employer what you are capable of. If you can show that you have initiative and can generate results on your own, so much the better. Being able to lead a team of people shows management skills and the ability to communicate well! Employers also like people who can work as a team member, so if you are not a team leader, but are a good team player, this is a point in your favour. Sentences which can make your work seem positive and dynamic will contain the verbs *achieved, initiated, planned, started, devised, directed, set up, wrote, elected, organized, supervised, prepared, improved, increased, turned (sales) around, strengthened, spearheaded*, and many more like these.

Special Achievements

If you have more than two special achievements or awards to your name, mention these in a separate section. As well as special academic achievements, list awards that you won at school, or were given to you for any community work. Give also any responsible positions that you held, for example, if you were the treasurer of an annual fund-raising event in Hong Kong!

Not to Put in Your Résumé

Do not use the word "I" in your résumé, or at the very least, keep it to a minimum. Try to emphasize what it was that you achieved, rather than the "I" that achieved it. For example, do not write, "I managed to turn the sales figures around for fiscal year 1992–93." Instead, write "turned around the sales figures for the fiscal year 1992–93." (See résumé examples).

There are certain items of information about yourself which you should never put into your résumé. These are your height, your weight, if you are single, married or engaged to be married, the number of children you have, your race, your religion, your sexual orientation or your health.

None of this information has anything to do with your ability to do the job in question and is simply not necessary. Similarly, your Hong Kong identity number at this stage is unnecessary, and enclosing a photograph is also unnecessary unless the job advertisement asks for it.

Never supply the names of your references on your résumé — simply state "References Available on Request." If an employer is seriously interested in you, he will ask you for your references and for your permission for him or her to contact them.

Reasons for leaving past jobs should never be given in your résumé. Your résumé should be a professional summary of your education, qualifications, work experience, strengths and special abilities.

And although many job advertisements in Hong Kong ask you to state your expected salary, it is best *not to give* the salary you expect until you are shortlisted and interviewed. If you have sold yourself well at the interview, the employer will be more than interested in you at this stage, and the issue of the salary you expect will be easier to discuss then. In many cases, the employer will not have set a fixed salary for the job in question and will be open to negotiation if he or she likes you a lot. Don't worry! If your résumé is strong, the employer will ask you to interview even if you have not mentioned your expected salary.

Your Final Draft

Your finished résumé must be right up-to-date. As you will be applying for many jobs at the same time, you may have to rewrite each a little differently for individual jobs, because of course job requirements will not be identical, and you will be tailoring your résumé to each job in question. At all times make sure that all dates are correct. Make sure you can explain any gaps between dates, if the reasons for the gaps are not given in your résumé. Never, never lie in your résumé, making your abilities seem greater than they are. You will be found out at interview, for sure. Do not give false information about previous jobs, as this will probably be checked, and again, you will be found out.

Constantly review your résumé, looking for ways to improve the way you express your sentences. Avoid clumsy wording. For example, instead of saying "Was in charge of an office of five people," write "Ran an office of five." Ask a native English speaker to look over your finished résumé, preferably someone with good writing skills! It is extremely important that your résumé is perfect.

Your final document must be typed, preferably using a computer, with a high-quality printer. The more professional you can make your résumé look, the better. Always type the address on the envelope containing your application. Never handwrite it.

Finally, you and you alone must write your résumé. No one knows you better than you. Do not be tempted to ask someone else to write your résumé for you.

The Application Form

Some companies ask you to fill in a standard application form. This makes it easier for the employer to compare applicants' information, but it is very restricting for you, as you are even less free to present your information in the way you want, and there may not even be sections you want to create on application forms.

Because of this, it is a good idea to send your résumé and your covering letter to the employer along with the completed application form.

Complete an application form in capital letters and in ink. If any section does not apply to you, write "Not Applicable." If there is a section which asks you to state your expected salary, write "Negotiable," or, worse, if you are asked to state your present salary, write "Confidential." For women, you are often asked to choose from "Mrs./Miss/Ms." This is sexist, as all men are simply "Mr." You can choose to ignore this section, also any section which asks for your marital status. Whether you are married or not has nothing to do with how well you would be able to do the job in question.

The Covering Letter

Your résumé is not the only document which you send to an employer.

You must also enclose a covering letter, which acts as a support for your résumé.

A covering letter is a supporting tool for you to use in order to sell yourself to an employer. Its purpose is to tell again how your strengths will be of benefit to the employer and the company, to help you to get an interview. Like your résumé, your covering letter must be better than the covering letters of the other applicants. A strong covering letter can make an employer decide to interview you while rejecting others, and keep you strongly in his or her mind during the interview.

A covering letter can be brief, or longer, depending on how much you feel you need to detail the benefits to the employer by hiring you.

Find out the name of the person who will be reading your résumé and covering letter, and address your letter to this person. If this name is not given in the job advertisement, telephone the company and find out. Be careful to ask for the correct spelling of the person's full name, and his or her title. The first paragraph of your covering letter is important, because if it is weak, the reader may not want to continue reading it. It must grab the attention of the reader and make him or her want to continue, want to interview you, and want to employ you!

Covering Letter for a Job Advertisement

If you are replying to a job advertisement, begin your covering letter by saying which job you are applying for and the name and the date of the publication it appeared in.

There are three main points in a covering letter. The first is that you should consider yourself as a product that you are trying to sell and so you should make a statement about how good you are and how the reader and the company would benefit by employing you. The second point is that you must prove that statement. Finally, the third point is that you must persuade or ask the reader to take action if he or she is interested in you.

A common mistake people make in their covering letters is to announce how they think the company or position advertised can benefit them. For example, they will write "I believe the position will be a positive challenge to me" — this is wrong! You should focus on the exact opposite — how you can be of benefit to the company! The "body" of your covering letter should point out your strengths and how they would be an asset to the employer and the company, without repeating what the employer can see in your résumé. If you have not yet completed your studies, you can point out how your expected qualifications and any student activities you were involved in can benefit the employer. Always, throughout your covering letter, emphasize that you would be good for the employer, and you need to prove (show) in your letter how you would be good for him or her. If you can fill the needs of the employer more than the other applicants, you will get the job. It's that simple. And in your covering letter, you need to make the employer feel that it seems like you can. Finally, you need to ask the employer for an interview, that is, persuade him or her to call you. State once again, briefly and in other words, how you would be of benefit to him or her, giving the best times for him or her to call you, along with your telephone number.

Note the following points of a covering letter for an advertised job:

1. Your letter should catch the attention of the reader.
2. Your letter should make him or her see very quickly how good you are.
3. Your letter should show very clearly that employing you would be a benefit to the company — that you fill the employer's needs.
4. Your letter should show proof to support the above.
5. Your letter should persuade the employer to take action (call you).

Look at the following letter. It is a covering letter to go with the chronological résumé we looked at above, in applying for an advertised job, and shows all the points summarized.

Flat A, 19/F
Victory Court
888 Poon Wah Street
Kowloon
Hong Kong

15th May 1998

Mr. P. K. Siu
Personnel Director
Telson plc.
134–136 Waterford Road
Kowloon Bay
Hong Kong

Dear Mr. Siu,

I refer to your advertisement for a Regional Sales Director in the *Hong Kong News*, Saturday, 15th May 1998. With my expertise in Sales Management, I believe I have much to offer Telson both in Hong Kong and throughout the Asia-Pacific region.

As you will see from my résumé, on the strength of my sales abilities from the beginning of my career to the present date, I have quickly reached the position of Senior Sales Manager in just six short years. I have a strong working knowledge of the markets of Japan, Korea, Taiwan, Malaysia, Singapore, Thailand and China, and I believe that my strong people skills and superior sales abilities would be a distinct asset to Telson as Regional Sales Director.

Please call me on 23456789 to arrange an interview — I will be happy to discuss with you in person how my skills and capabilities would be perfectly suited to the advertised position of Regional Sales Director, and how I would be of benefit to Telson.

Yours sincerely,

WONG Kam Wah James

Prospecting a Company for a Job

It is often a good idea to send your résumé and covering letter to a company to find out if they have any job openings in the field you are looking in. This is called prospecting for a job. If you do this, again, find out the name of the Senior Personnel Manager (call the company — the receptionist should be able to tell you) and address your letter to him or her. This can impress an employer as it shows that you can take initiative. Of course also ask for the complete address. Remember to type the address on the envelope, never write it by hand.

As you do not know whether or not there would be a job for you in the company, your covering letter should show an interest in the company, and also show that you know the business of the company. To do this, you need to do some research into the company. This shows the reader that you have taken the trouble to find out about the company. As with an advertised job, you should again state how you would be of benefit to the company if they were to employ you. Again, if you have not yet completed your studies, make the employer know how, when you obtain your degree, you could be of benefit to him or her. Mention any student activities you were/are involved in which would also show him or her that you would be a benefit to the company. For example, if you want to go into journalism, you could state, "Editor of *StuRag*, our monthly student magazine."

When prospecting for a job, the same as when replying to a job advertisement, you must win the attention of the reader of your letter immediately. Following that, you must state that you are good. Next, you have to support that statement — you have to prove, or show it in your letter. Finally, you have to persuade the reader to take action (call you) if he or she is interested in what you have to offer. Ask for an interview. When prospecting for a job, it is acceptable to tell the employer that *you* will be calling *him or her*, and give a day and a time when you will be calling. (To allow the employer to be prepared for your call.) This shows the employer that you can take control of a situation, and that you show initiative, which is an advantage to you. More than ever, your covering letter in a prospecting letter will have to work to sell you.

Note the following points of a covering letter when prospecting for a job:

1. Your letter should catch the attention of the reader.
2. Your letter should very quickly make him or her see how good you are.
3. Your letter should show very clearly that employing you would be a benefit to the company — that you fill the employer's needs.
4. Your letter should show proof to support the above.
5. Your letter should persuade the employer to take action (call you), or tell him what action you are going to take (call or visit him or her).

Look at this example of a prospecting letter written by James Wong to Telson plc. It shows all the points summarized.

✍

Flat A, 19/F
Victory Court
888 Poon Wah Street
Kowloon
Hong Kong

8th February 1998

Mr. P. K. Siu
Personnel Director
Telson plc.
134–136 Waterford Road
Kowloon Bay
Hong Kong

Dear Mr. Siu,

The business section in the *Hong Kong News*, Thursday, 8th February 1998, reports that Telson plc. is rapidly expanding into the Asia-Pacific region.

I am a dynamic, aggressive and results-oriented individual in Senior Sales Management, now looking for an opening with Telson, where I believe my unique skills would be of noticeable benefit to your company.

As you will see from my résumé, I have reached the position of Senior Sales Manager in only six short years. I have consistently achieved and exceeded all sales targets throughout my career, and strongly turned around falling sales figures.

I also have a strong working knowledge of the markets of Japan, Korea, Taiwan, Malaysia, Thailand, Singapore and China, which would be a great asset to Telson's projected expansion into the Asia-Pacific region.

Please refer to my résumé for additional information regarding my working experience, education and achievements.

I will telephone you on Monday morning of next week (12th of February) when I trust we can arrange an interview. I will be happy to discuss with you in person how my skills and capabilities would be of benefit to Telson.

Yours sincerely,

WONG Kam Wah James

Following-up Your Application

You have written the very best résumé you can, with a great covering letter which, you feel, cannot fail to get you to an interview. Yet two weeks or more pass without a call or a letter from the employer.... In a situation like this, it is a good idea to write a short letter reminding the employer that you are still very much interested in working for him or her. In Hong Kong, many employers state in their job advertisements that unsuccessful candidates will not be notified, and no news will mean that you were unsuccessful. However, if this was one job that you were very eager to have, a follow-up letter can still work in your favour. It shows the employer that you are seriously interested in working for him or her, and, by reminding him or her of the benefits you will bring to the company, the employer may well consider you again, especially as in Hong Kong, staff turnover rate is extremely high compared to other parts of the world. This may mean that the person who was offered the job may leave before too long, and, if you are persistent, the employer may decide to interview you.

Here is an example of a follow-up letter to your written application.

Dear Mr. Siu,

Three weeks ago I applied for the advertised position of Regional Sales Director with Telson. I would like to advise you that I am still extremely interested in offering my skills for the benefit of the Telson company.

I strongly believe that my experience in sales in the Asia-Pacific region would bring significant benefits to your company. I look forward to discussing what my potential can do for Telson — I will telephone in the morning of this coming Monday 8th of March when we may discuss the possibility of arranging an interview.

Yours sincerely,

WONG Kam Wah James

After the Interview

Congratulations! You have been invited to interview, and have given your best sales talk outlining how your services could be of benefit to the company. If the interviewer is very impressed with you, he or she will probably offer you the job on the spot. However in most cases, he will have other candidates to interview and you will have to wait to see if you are on the short list.

Immediately after the interview, send the employer a short message of thanks. This will surprise him or her, because other applicants will not think to do this, especially in Hong Kong! Your politeness will be remembered. This short thank-you letter will also remind him or her of who you are, and it may be enough to make him or her make up his or her mind to either interview you again, or offer you the job, especially if you briefly cover again how your strengths will benefit him or her by employing you.

Here is an example of such a thank-you letter.

✍🏻

Dear Mr. Siu,

Thank you for taking the time to discuss with me at interview how my skills, strengths and qualifications would be of particular benefit to Telson should I be chosen for the post of Regional Sales Director, recently advertised.

I enjoyed meeting you and learning even more about the Telson company.

I now feel even more confident that my achievements, skills and strengths are particularly suited to the post and that the benefits to Telson by employing me would be great. In particular, I would enjoy the challenge of not only meeting but exceeding your sales quotas in the foreign markets we discussed. The results of my past achievements in this field speak for themselves.

I look forward to hearing from you soon.

Yours sincerely,

WONG Kam Wah James

After an Unsuccessful Application

Even if you got as far as an interview but were rejected, you can still write a follow-up letter which may turn the situation around for you.

Employers are always very surprised to receive a letter following a rejection, because it really shows that you were very interested in the job in question. If nothing else, your persistence will be admired. This kind of letter can be very similar to the follow-up letter you would write if you have had no reply after sending your résumé and covering letter, and you may well be offered the job for the same reasons as mentioned above — that is, the person who did get the job may not stay long ... or the employer may be so impressed with your politeness, interest in the job and persistence that he will create a similar job for you (or even dismiss the "successful" applicant, whose performance is not as good as yours seems!).

Here is an example of a follow-up letter to an unsuccessful interview.

Dear Mr. Siu,

I was very disappointed to learn that I was not chosen for the post of Regional Sales Director for Telson. Thank you for contacting me so promptly with the news.

I am still most interested in an opening at this level in management with your company. I strongly feel that, with my expertise, skills, drive and dynamism, I could bring many benefits to Telson — the requirements for the post of Regional Sales Director lay well within my capabilities.

I would like to contact you again in a month's time to discuss possible openings which may have arisen in the company. In the meantime, please keep my résumé and covering letter on file.

Many thanks.

Yours sincerely,

WONG Kam Wah James

The Interview

It is easy to feel nervous at an interview, especially if you really want the job on offer, because you know that you will have to sell yourself very well, better, in fact, than any of the other applicants.

The interviewer will be trying to eliminate you — several

applicants are short-listed and a process of elimination begins, where the interviewer will try to find reasons for not giving you the job. You, on the other hand, have to highlight your strengths, make even your weaknesses sound positive, and give him or her good reasons for recruiting you — the benefit you would be to the company.

Be Prepared Before the Day

You can do a lot to make sure that the interview will go in your favour. Before the day of the interview, it is sensible to make a trip to the building so that you will be able to find it easily on the day, and you will know how long it will take you to get there. On the day, arrive early, find a restroom and make sure you look good.

You should find out everything you can about the company (how it operates, and its products) before the day of the interview. A good library will have this information up-to-date, the Chamber of Commerce certainly will. If the company you are applying to is a foreign company in Hong Kong, visit the Chamber of Commerce for that country here. If you have time, write to or fax the headquarters of the company abroad.

Find out also, if possible, the name and title of the person who will be interviewing you.

Find out if you will be sitting any tests and what kind of tests these will be, because this will give you better time to prepare. Find out if you are to be interviewed by one person or by a panel of people.

Find out as much as you can about the job advertised before the day of the interview. Why is the job being advertised? What career developments are available to someone in this job? What is the salary range for this kind of job?

Prepare a list of possible questions the employer could ask you, and supply answers to these questions. Ask a friend or family member to ask you these questions and practise answering them. Common difficult questions asked in interviews are given below:

1. **What makes you think you are the best candidate for the job?**
   Here, sell yourself! Give your strengths *which are related to the job in question*. Use achievements from previous employment or

university or college. State clearly how the employer would benefit by hiring you.

2. **What do you see yourself doing five years from now?**

   Think seriously about the answer to this question, because you may be asked it. You can say something like, "I expect to be in middle/upper management in a company like this one."

3. **Why are you looking for a new job?**

   "I feel that I can do no more for my present company — I'm looking to expand my skills in a company where I can make a greater contribution."

4. **Why did you apply for this job?**

   Here, show what you know about the company from your research. Tell the interviewer how you can benefit the company based on what you know about it.

5. **Why have you changed jobs three times in the past five years?**

   "I believed that my strengths and skills were not being used to their full advantage by previous employers."

6. **How are we to know that you won't leave us in a year's time?**

   "This company is well-valued by its employees. I believe that here the benefits I could give to the company will be well valued."

7. **How long do you think you will stay in this job?**

   "As long as I feel I am making a valued contribution to the company."

8. **What kind of people do you find difficult to work with?**

   "I get impatient with lazy people, but in general I try to work well with all kinds of people."

9. **How much do you know about our company?**

   Here, again, use your research! Tell all that you have found out about the company.

10. **Do you know the name of the Chairperson of our company?**

    "Of course! It's Mr./Mrs. (give full name)."

11. **Tell me what benefit you would be to this company.**

    Here, really focus on your strong points and achievements and match them to the job in question — sell yourself as strongly as possible.

12. **Tell me how you have shown initiative in your past employment.**

This is an important question if you are being interviewed for work with a Western company — Western bosses complain that lack of initiative is the biggest weakness among Hong Kong staff. In answer to this question, you must state clearly any work-related situations in which you have made decisions on your own and acted on these decisions alone.

13. **Tell me how you have demonstrated problem-solving abilities in your past employment.**

Here, tell the interviewer any work-related occasions in the past when you were the key person to solving a problem.

14. **What have you not liked about your past/present bosses?**

By asking this question, the interviewer is trying to find out if you are the kind of person who would say negative things about others. If you can say negative things about your past or present bosses, the interviewer will be sure that you will do the same for this new company and its bosses. Never, in any interview, say anything negative about your previous company, bosses, employees, teachers etc. To answer this one, look surprised, and say, "I have always liked all of my bosses!"

15. **What do you think are your weak points?**

Never tell an employer what your weak points are! If necessary, hide them behind strong statements. Say, "Well, I am a perfectionist," or, "I guess I expect a lot from the people I work with."

Make a list of questions to ask the interviewer. He or she will probably invite you to ask questions of your own towards the end of the interview. Never say that you have no questions. Questions show that you are curious, interested, and stimulated by the discussion. Ask questions on possible career paths for the successful applicant, potential for promotion within the company for the successful applicant, and if there would be any special courses or training available. You can also say, "Well, I was going to ask you about (topic), but we talked about that earlier."

Before the day of the interview, think about your strong points. You have to use these strong points to sell yourself during the interview. List all your past achievements which may be relevant to the job in question.

Learn your strengths and achievements by heart and be sure to mention them at appropriate points throughout the interview.

Be sure to dress smartly and be well-groomed. Have a hair cut and look clean and tidy. Best colours to wear to an interview are dark greys and dark blues — women as well as men should wear a suit. Women should keep make-up and nail colour very natural, tights (pantyhose) should be black, and not glossy.

At the Interview

Arrive early. When invited into the interview room, smile and make eye contact, shake the interviewer's hand firmly, but do not crush his bones.

Some interviewers arrange several chairs in the room and invite you to sit. Your choice of chair says a lot about you. Your best choice is to sit in the chair that will put you closest to the interviewer, with your head at the same level as his or hers. If he or she is still standing while asking you to sit, invite him or her to sit first!

Relax — the first few minutes will be small talk. An experienced interviewer will have made an impression of you — good or bad — in the first four minutes of meeting you. His impression of you will be good if you are yourself, and give signs of confidence. Sit back into the chair but sit up, lean forward slightly, and keep still. Face the interviewer squarely and do not cross your arms if your legs are crossed. Do not play with a small object on his or her desk or fiddle with a ring or your watch, etc. Keep your hands still in your lap.

Look the interviewer in the eyes all the time he or she is speaking to you.

When you are speaking to the interviewer, maintain regular eye contact while occasionally glancing away. Smile warmly where appropriate. Give the interviewer the feeling that you are a nice person to know. If he or she has a good feeling about you in the first few minutes, his or her final decision will be influenced by this first impression.

Your whole focus should be on your strengths and on being positive. Every sentence you say should be a positive one, with emphasis on the benefits to the employer/the company if you get the job. Look at the following sentences. You will see how to make strong, positive sentences from negative, or weaker ones.

Examples.

Do not say	Say
I have never learned XYZ computer skills.	I am competent with ABC and DEF computer skills, so learning XYZ will not be a problem for me.
This would be my first job in management, and I would need some guidance at first.	At university I successfully lead a team of twelve people in our final-year market research programme. I strongly feel that my management skills would be of significant benefit to your department.
I'm not sure that my English is good enough for communication with English-speaking customers.	Learning English to fluency will not be a problem for me.

Talking about Salary

The only reason you get out of bed and go to work in the morning is because you get paid for it. Salary is important to everyone — and you need to know how to negotiate for the amount you want without being greedy. As mentioned earlier in this chapter, you should never mention your expected salary before you get into an interview. If the company telephones you to say that you forgot to mention it in your application and could you please tell them now, refuse, saying that it is something you would prefer to discuss at the interview.

One of the questions you could ask during the interview is the salary which is being offered with the job. (Normally, salary is discussed towards the end of the interview.) When the interviewer tells you, you will be able to compare it with your present salary. Ask if the salary is negotiable, and about any bonuses given. The interviewer will not negotiate the salary with you unless you are offered the job, and you should not mention the salary you are getting until you are offered the job! If the interviewer offers the job to you, that is the time to begin salary negotiation, and you are more in a position to control the negotiation.

Interviewing in English

Most interviews in Hong Kong are in Cantonese. However, with some higher-level jobs, you will be expected to give some or all of the interview in English. And of course, interviews for Western companies will normally be all in English.

It is not easy expressing yourself in an interview in a language which is not your own. To achieve the best results, use words which are familiar to you and keep your sentences short and simple. It is not necessary to use long words which sound impressive. What is important is your confidence in your ability to be a benefit to the company. Speak slowly and clearly, making sure that your pronunciation is the best you can give. If you are being interviewed by an English-speaking Westerner, you might feel like a fish out of water before his or her fluent, easy English. But be assured that most Westerners admire your ability to be able to communicate in English — no matter how poor your English sounds to you! And you can be sure that your English-speaking interviewer is very unlikely to be able to speak Cantonese as well as you have mastered English, and he or she will be aware of that! So relax and enjoy your English interview.

Your Body Communicates Too

The way your body communicates to the interviewer is important too.

Remember, never cross your arms (says that you are feeling unfriendly), or lean back in your chair with your hands behind your head (says that you are feeling superior to the interviewer). Keep your upper body facing the interviewer with your hands resting in your lap if you are not talking. It is acceptable to use your hands to help you to express yourself when you are talking. It is very important to keep quite still — do not swing your leg, for example, or shake your foot. Although they may seem like little movements to you, to the interviewer they are very noticeable.

Sit up in your chair and lean forward slightly. Putting your head on one side as the interviewer talks to you tells him or her that you are listening attentively. If you can remember to copy your interviewer's basic body language, almost like a mirror reflection, this will work for you. There is no need to scratch your nose when the interviewer scratches his or hers, but if you can try to copy his or her basic arm, leg and head movements, he or she will find himself or herself liking you and not really knowing why …

Some Final Words of Advice

If the interviewer is a woman, and you are a man, do not think that you can be less careful about what you say or how you behave. A woman interviewer will be more aware of your attitude than any man, and, if you seriously want the job, you need to treat her seriously too.

Never smoke, or chew gum during the interview.

Never argue with the interviewer — doing this will cost you the job. If you disagree with anything he or she says, be assertive and polite, even friendly.

Afterwards

Most of us leave the interview room annoyed with ourselves for forgetting to say this, or by not saying that in a better way, or for making what we think is a mess of what we intended to say well. As soon as possible after the interview, it is a good idea to make notes on what you felt went badly, as well as on what you thought were good points during the interview. This will help you in future interviews — you learn from your mistakes, and as you become more experienced with the interview game, you will not make the same mistakes in future.

As mentioned earlier in this chapter, write a short follow-up letter to the person who interviewed you, thanking the interviewer for the interview which you enjoyed. This step is rarely done in Hong Kong and may even tip the balance in your favour if you were already a possibility for the job in his or her mind.

Exercise I

A. Rewrite the following badly written covering letter.

Dear Sir,

I am writing to you to apply for the job I saw in the newspaper. You will find my résumé with this letter. If you look at my résumé you will see that I have the right qualifications and experience for the job you advertised. I think that your company could have a lot to offer me and I would be very happy to work for you so that I can grow in my career. I would like you to interview me so that you can see for yourself how your company would be good for me. You can call me anytime. Thank you very much.

B. Rewrite the following badly written prospecting letter.

Dear Sir,

I am writing to you to ask if you have a job for me in your company. I am very boring in the job I have at the moment and I am looking for another job. My friend told me that your company is a good company to work for and so I am writing this letter to you. I have sent you my résumé with this letter. If you look at my résumé you will see what I am good at. I have lots of experience in many things and I am sure that if you can give me a job, it will be very good for me in my career. I am going to call you next week because I want you to interview me.

C. Rewrite the following badly written follow-up letter.

Dear Sir,

Three weeks ago I sent you my résumé and a letter because I wanted to apply for the job that you advertised in the newspaper. But, I have heard nothing from you. I really want the job and I hope that you will consider me. I will be very disappointed if I do not get the job. I am going to call you on Monday to find out what is happening. I still think I am the best person for the job and I think that working for your company will be very good for me in my career.

D. Rewrite the following badly written follow-up letter to an unsuccessful application.

Dear Sir,

I am just writing to tell you that I am very upset that you did not give me the job. I think I am the best person for the job and that a job in your company would be very good for me in my career. I really really wanted that job and I think that I could do the job better than anybody else. I would be very happy if you would interview me again so that you can see how your company would be good for me if you employ me. I am going to telephone you on Monday so that we can set a date for an interview.

Thank you.

Exercise II

1. Students split into pairs. Swop résumés and covering letters. Take home your partner's résumé and covering letter and state what you would consider to be improvements.
2. Students split into pairs with their partners. Discuss the suggestions for improvement the other has made at home. Accept or reject, with reasons.

Task I

In yours pairs, interview each other using the completed résumés and covering letters.

Each pair writes their names on a small piece of paper. All papers are folded and put into a small jar. Five pairs are drawn. These pairs are to do their interviews in front of the class. The observers are asked to take notes, positive and negative, on the interviewee, body language, responses, confidence etc., and to give their observations at the end. The observers are asked — would you employ this person? Why/why not?

Task II

You have seen a job advertised that you are really interested in. Write your own résumé and covering letter for this job.

12

Speaking and Listening

In this chapter, you will learn:

- how to speak effectively in presentations and meetings;
- how to give and receive telephone calls and voice mail messages productively;
- how to really listen to others.

People who are effective in both business, and also in their private lives, are good communicators. But as we have seen, communication is not only about writing,. and reading what is written. Communication also includes speaking and listening, both of which are very important.

It is easy to develop writing skills, but the other skills should also be worked on, especially the skill of listening, which we sometimes feel is not so important at all.

Poor Listening

Not listening effectively can cost your company money. Rewritten messages, repeat telephone calls, redirected shipments and date and deadline changes can all result because the person who was supposed to process the information was not listening well enough. People do not listen well for several reasons. They include:

1. Physical handicaps — Hearing impairments or a noisy background

can prevent a person from hearing well. If a person is sick, worried, in shock, in pain or tired, he or she will not listen well.

2. Uninteresting information — Not all people find the same information interesting. A lecture on any subject, for example, would be deadly boring to many people, yet extremely interesting to just as many. If a person does not find the subject interesting, or if he or she thinks that he or she does not need the information or that it will be of no use, then he or she will not listen well.

3. Language problems — People who cannot fluently understand the language that is being spoken to them will not be able to listen well. Words, phrases or whole sentences may be missed. Nuances of tone will not be picked up, and their associated meanings will be lost. Furthermore, some words have a very deep meaning to some people. For example "euthanasia" may make the listener react so strongly emotionally that he or she will not hear the words that follow.

4. Physical distractions — If the speaker has an odd characteristic, like blue hair or no arms, the listener will not listen well. Similarly if the listener is distracted by people walking across the room or by something else he or she sees going on nearby, listening will be lessened.

5. Speed of thought vs. speed of speech — Our thoughts are racing all the time. Compared to the speed of the speech of the speaker, our minds may be way off track. If the speaker speaks very slowly, the listener may "switch off" altogether. In both cases, the listener will not listen well.

6. Pretending to listen — Most of us have pretended to listen even when we are not listening. This is damaging in the long run, because if the listener pretends to be listening very often, he or she will find it difficult to concentrate when he or she does want to listen. Therefore the listener cannot listen well.

7. Waiting, not listening — Your opinions and experiences are very important to you. Most of us would prefer to talk than listen to somebody else talking. The result is that we wait for the other person to finish a sentence before cutting in with what we have to say. We concentrate on grabbing the space rather than on listening

to what the speaker has said. If we spend time in conversation waiting like this, then we will not listen well.

In order to improve listening, you can remove the above problems by focusing on the following skills.

Learn to Listen

1. Shut up — Let the other person talk, and really concentrate on what he or she is saying. Ask questions to help him or her continue. If you are meant to talk, you will be asked a question. If nobody asks you a question, listen to what is being said.

2. Do not talk when others are talking — How many times have you been sitting around a table with several other people and two or more of the group have been talking all at the same time? This is a situation which is disastrous for listening, and gives an "only what I have to say is important" message. Let one person at a time talk, the rest listen.

3. Get rid of background noise — Hong Kong is an exceptionally noisy place, which is unfortunate for sharpening listening skills. In order to listen most effectively, you need silence. Close the windows, get away from noisy chatter, switch off radios, pagers, mobile phones and televisions.

4. Be positive — Expect to learn something from what you hear, instead of negatively switching off because what is being said is uninteresting to you. Concentrate and stretch your mind if the subject is difficult for you to understand.

5. Pick out the main ideas as you listen — This will help you to understand and consolidate what is being said.

6. Instead of letting your mind wander as the speaker speaks, try to think what he or she will say next — Bring everything he or she has already said into the total picture of your understanding of the speech.

7. Listen for the feelings — In English, intonation and tone are extremely important in the delivery and understanding of a message. Concentrate on understanding what is really being said. Likewise,

in English, sometimes what is not said is often as important as what is spoken. Learn to "hear" what is not said.

8. Ignore the physical — If the physical appearance of the speaker is strange, be extra attentive to what he or she is saying. Make an extra effort to concentrate if people are walking in and out around you or if there are nearby physical distractions.

9. Do not argue — Let the other person give his or her side of the argument first, and listen to it carefully. This will give you a chance to evaluate and understand what the other person has said, before you put your point(s) across.

10. Take notes of the main points — In some situations, it is wise to note the main points of what is being said, to refer to again later. Jot down only the important points. Trying to write down everything the speaker says will detract from your listening potential.

11. Show that you are listening — Keep your eyes contact with speaker. Make brief comments at appropriate times, smile, nod, shake your head, and ask questions. Nothing is worse than a speaker realizing that the person or people he or she is talking to is/are not listening. It is also extremely rude.

Use feedback to confirm understanding

The Spoken Report

In business, speaking skills are very important. You may have to give presentations regularly, depending on what position you hold and what job you do. If you are in sales, your speaking skills will be vital to you. In many managerial positions, you will be required to explain, describe, clarify, convince and persuade almost daily. As you grow in your career, so must your speaking skills.

Speaking to a small informal group, or to a large formal audience is something that every business executive will have to face sooner or later in his or her career. As with written reports, thorough planning is very important.

Think about Your Audience

Gather together as much information about your audience as you possibly can. In general, a large audience will require a more formal approach, a small group much more informal. Find out the age, sex, race(s) and number of people in your audience. Know what their attitude will be to your subject, and their level of knowledge of it. Ask yourself the following questions before you start:

1. How is the audience likely to react to my subject?
2. What is the purpose of giving my speech?
3. Do I want the audience to take any action after my speech?
4. Which parts of my speech will be most interesting to the audience?
5. What visual aids will be most effective in presenting my information?

Arranging the Content

As with written reports, begin your spoken report by thinking about and pinpointing the reason for it. Do you want to use it to persuade or to inform, or to make a suggestion? Before you begin to write your report, write a statement which gives the reason. As with written reports, this is called the purpose statement, and it is the goal of your report. It will focus your writing and help you to organize it. For example:

✍🏻

To inform all product managers of the new China policy.

To persuade upper management that an amalgamation of the China office would increase efficiency.

To recommend the downsizing of the Tokyo office to upper management.

After writing a good purpose statement, arrange your spoken report so that it leads towards your goal. Spoken reports may follow either the direct or the indirect method. As you will remember, the direct method is used when you expect the receiver to react in a neutral or a pleased manner. The direct method states the main idea first, followed by reasons and explanations. The indirect method gives reasons and explanations first, followed by the main idea. This method is used if you expect the receiver to be upset or angry by the main idea, or at least to show some resistance to it.

Most spoken reports are delivered using the indirect method. This is because the listeners will not, in most cases, know anything about the main idea and will need explanations and reasons beforehand. You will need to make rough guidelines to help you to organize your report. These guidelines should focus on only a few main points.

Spoken presentations also follow the format of an introduction, a body, and the conclusion or summary. Receivers of written reports can re-read what has been said and can also control the speed at which they read. Listeners of reports cannot control the speed of delivery, nor can they re-read the main points. Good speakers know this, and so they speak slowly, carefully and clearly, and recap the main points or ideas several times for the benefit of their listeners. Good speakers also give their listeners a preview of what they are going to be told, as well as reviews of what has been said. Good speakers also make easy-to-follow transitions between the parts of their spoken report.

The Introduction

Introduce yourself at the beginning of your speech if your listeners do not know who you are. You may well have been introduced by another person who has told the audience a few sentences about you. If this is the case, there is no need to introduce yourself. Say what you are going to be talking about. Give a brief outline of what you will be covering. Use an attention-grabbing tactic with your listeners at the beginning of your report, for example, ask a question (which you may like to answer in the summary), tell a joke, give a quotation or a surprising fact. Your attention-grabber should, ideally, be related to your speech.

The Body

When preparing your speech of the report, you have to organize the content into a few important points. In the body of your report, present these now, in logical order. Give supporting ideas for each main point. Your supporting ideas should be brief and not too detailed — your listeners will not be able to absorb a great many facts. As you progress through speech, summarize each main point, for example:

It is clear, then, that by amalgamating with the Shenzhen office, we will be able to reduce costs and increase efficiency.

Always refer back to what you have said, and try to link what you have said with what you are about to say. For example:

I've talked about amalgamation with the Shenzhen office. Now let's look at possible amalgamation with Panyu.

I've mentioned three good reasons for the amalgamation with Panyu, but the reason I'm going to cover now is perhaps the most valid.

Help the listener to clarify in his or her mind the main points of your spoken report, and the connections between them, by reporting these main ideas often as you go through your speech, and by the use of effective transitional words and/or phrases, e.g., so, then, next, following that, after that, therefore, however, etc.

The Conclusion

Your presentation may conclude with either a summary, if the content of the presentation is mainly informative, or with a conclusion if the report is an analysis of data. Either way, include a revision of the presentation's main ideas. Remember your purpose statement — focus on a conclusion that will help to achieve that goal. If your introduction began with a question as an attention-grabber, answer that question now. Ask your listeners if they have any questions. If not, tell them that you will be happy to answer questions on a one-to-one basis later.

Aids to Help You

Your listeners will remember your report much more easily if you use visual aids. Pictures, drawings, charts, graphs, etc. can be used to emphasize your message so that your listeners will better retain what you say.

In spoken reports, the usual visual aids are transparencies, whiteboard, flip papers, slides and handouts.

Transparencies are popular because they can be prepared in advance, and, as the screen used to show them can be large, the information on it can be seen by everyone in a large audience. Transparencies are often used to give main points or ideas, and are useful to the speaker as they help him or her to remember the outline of the presentation.

A whiteboard is another useful visual aid, especially if it is elevated for a larger audience to see. The disadvantage is that erasing information to make space for new items can be distracting.

Flip papers are more efficient than whiteboards for that reason — there is no need to erase. When you finish one page, flip it over to the back and start a new page. However, flip papers are not so effective if you have a large group of listeners as many may not be able to see.

Slides are useful for picture presentations, for example, taking your audience around a new factory or plant. For best results, you should coordinate your presentation with someone who will operate the slide projector for you. You can, of course, operate the machine yourself as you give your presentation. Keep slide presentations short — in a darkened room, your audience may fall asleep — is it necessary to point this out? Not necessary!

Handouts should ideally be given to your audience at the end of your presentation. This stops them from reading when they should be listening to you. The content of handouts should be information that helps to make the report clear.

To make your visual aids the most effective for your listeners, use them only to emphasize important points, or to clarify important information. Keep your information visually simple and uncluttered, and make sure the equipment works. Just before your audience arrives, try out the slide projector and/or any sound system. Make sure that every person can see the screen, flip paper or whiteboard; move microphone stands etc. if necessary, and remember to face and talk to your listeners. Do not address the screen, board or flip paper!

Giving the Report

There are certain techniques used by experienced speakers to catch and hold the attention of their listeners, and these can be learned by anyone. Even if the information in your report is interesting, and you have prepared your spoken report extremely carefully, your listeners will not give you their full attention if you do not present it well.

Your speech needs to sound natural, and it also needs to sound dynamic. Weak, unnaturally sound speech will quickly cause listeners to lose their concentration and attention.

There are four ways of giving presentations. One way is to learn the whole presentation by heart. Although it may make you feel more secure, this way is not to be recommended because it will sound false and your listeners will know that you are just reciting from memory. Another disadvantage is that if you forget what comes next, especially if you are nervous, the entire presentation may collapse.

Another way is for you to read your report. However, if you have ever listened to a speaker reading everything, you will understand what an unfavourable impression this can create. Your listeners will not be impressed by your lack of confidence and lack of knowledge about your subject. Furthermore, listening to a speaker who has no eye contact with his or her audience is very boring.

A third way of delivering a speech is talking from written clues. This method is the best — and most effective. In front of you on the lectern is a piece of paper with key sentences, based on the main points of what you have to say. These sentences are clues only, so you should know your topic very well. With this kind of spoken presentation, you will have to practise beforehand, using the notes you will use in your actual presentation. Aim to speak to your listeners in a conversational way, making it lively and natural.

The final way of presenting a spoken report is if you have to im-provise, that is, do it without prior preparation. You may be asked to give such a report by upper management, or you may suddenly have to explain something to your subordinates through a speech. It is not easy to deliver an oral report with no preparation, and obviously this method is not ideal. You will have to know your topic very well indeed; it helps if you can write down a few notes covering the main points in logical order.

Speaking before an Audience

It is normal to feel nervous. You can learn how to overcome nervousness and also how to present your speech for optimum effectiveness if you put the following success techniques into practice:

Before You Speak

1. Make sure you are very well prepared. Be very familiar with your subject and make an accurate outline.
2. Rehearse your presentation many times; record yourself if possible so that you can screen out anything unsatisfactory. Time yourself — 20–30 minutes is a good window.
3. Make sure you have a lectern. Use it for your notes, and on which to occasionally rest your arms or hands.
4. Before the audience arrives, make sure all your audio-visual equip-ment are in working order.
5. Breathe deeply before you are called upon to speak. Focus on your breathing and not on what is before you. This will calm any nerves.

Delivering Your Presentation

1. After stepping up to the lectern, pause. Compose yourself and your notes. Establish control.
2. Deliver the first sentence from memory. This will allow you to establish eye contact immediately with your listeners, which will catch their attention from the start. This confidence will also arouse positive impressions of you among the audience and your eye contact with them will reinforce this.
3. Tell them in the introduction that you will answer any questions at the end.
4. Keep eye contact throughout your presentation, except when dropping it to read your next key sentence.
5. Speak much more slowly than normal. Listen to well-known public deliver speeches, and note the speed of their delivery. Avoid making noises such as "um," "er," "ah," "uh," and avoid saying "you know" to your listeners. Stay silent instead.
6. Do not jingle money in your pockets or fiddle with anything else. Keep your body still, and move naturally when you want to move. If you are using a whiteboard or flip paper, move to and from it slowly and naturally.
7. Move to one side of the whiteboard or flip paper so that everyone can see. Using a pointer is a good idea.
8. Stay on track. Do not go off at a tangent if you suddenly think of something clever during your presentation.
9. At the end, give the summary or conclusion. Clarify the main points again, and, if necessary, emphasize what action you would like your listeners to take or what you would like them to believe.

Afterwards

1. Ask for questions, and give a time limit. For example, say "For the next ten minutes I will be happy to answer any questions."
2. If your audience is large, repeat each question so that everyone in the room will have heard it.
3. Do not ever argue with anyone in the audience. Answer all questions calmly and clearly.

4. Do not engage in a dialogue with just one listener.
5. Let the audience know that time is up. Thank them with the opportunity to talk with them.

Good Speaking and Listening Skills — The Key to Successful Meetings

Meetings are successful when (1) they are necessary (i.e., when memos, phone calls or one-to-one conversations would not be appropriate), (2) when they are well-planned, (3) when the person conducting the meeting has strong leadership skills, and (4) when all taking part in the meeting have good speaking and listening skills.

Necessary Meetings

Meetings are necessary when a memo, phone calls or conversations would not be the best way to achieve the goal. Think carefully before calling a meeting. Unnecessary meetings are a complete waste of everybody's time.

Plan the Meeting

You have to start with a plan. You need to begin by thinking of what your goal is — what you want to achieve by holding the meeting. When you have established the goal, write an agenda. This is simply a list of items which you want to cover in the meeting. Write the time you estimate each item will take to discuss, and the estimated time at which the meeting will end.

If another individual or individuals are to present one or more of the items, include their names. Each person who is to attend the meeting should receive the agenda at least two days before the date of the meeting. If the meeting is to be a long one, include refreshments.

Run It Well

Good leadership skills ensure successful meetings. One of the qualities of a good leader is to have effective communication skills. However, other skills shown by the leader will ensure a successful meeting. Here they are:

1. Start the meeting on time — Waiting for latecomers is disrespectful to those who are punctual. If your meetings start late, the attendees will always be late, sometimes very late. Those who are on time will be irritated having to wait for latecomers.
2. Begin your meetings with a very brief introduction which includes the meeting goals, duration, the problem which needs to be discussed, any feasible solutions and possible limitations of these solutions, and the proposed agenda. This should take a few minutes only, and you should then ask if everybody agrees with all of the above points.
3. Appoint somebody to take minutes.
4. Start the discussion and encourage members to participate. Make sure the meeting keeps to the agenda and also keeps on time. If the participants are off-track, bring them back. Encourage everybody to talk by asking the quiet ones questions: "James, what do you think?" or, "Belinda, how would you resolve it?" Do not allow the meeting to be controlled by one or two members with a dominating character. When there is agreement among the group, sum it up briefly and ask if all agree. End the meeting at the given time and say that a report of the meeting will be sent to all participants within a number of days.

Participate Well

If you are not leading the meeting but are attending as one of the participants, prepare for it. You should have received the agenda at least two days before the meeting date. Study it. Familiarize yourself with the problem and the ways to resolve it with their limitations.

Find out how the problem has been tackled before, and understand why other methods failed, or partially succeeded. Know that upper management will be aware of participants who excel at meetings and you will give yourself the opportunity to excel if you prepare thoroughly and take part effectively. In other words, careful preparation before and effective participation at meetings can earmark you for promotion.

Arrive at the location of the meeting five minutes before the start. Speak at the beginning if you want to, but wait until others have spoken too, so that you can form your opinions and ideas based on their ideas to your benefit.

Effective Telephone Communication

Using the telephone is only effective if it increases the productivity of the company. Otherwise, it is resource-wasting and causes bad feeling, neither of which contribute to a company's productivity.

Making Productive Telephone Calls

Before you even pick up the phone, think about whether it is even necessary to make the call. It is very true that the invention of the telephone has revolutionized business by its time-saving qualities alone, but on the other hand, receiving a call can interrupt the work of someone else which in fact lowers that person's/company's productivity. Perhaps you could find the information you want by yourself, so that you would not have to bother another person for it. Would the information reach you if you were to wait a while? Less disruptive methods of communication to another person are faxes, e-mails, memos or voice mails, which do not demand that you reply to them at once. It would be safe to say that, in business, the only calls that should be made should be urgent ones, or ones to which you really do need information immediately. The following is a list of ways to make your telephone calls most productive:

1. Write down a few notes on the items you want to cover before you pick up the phone. In this way, you will not forget any item and embarrass yourself by having to call the person back and disturb him or her again.
2. Give three pieces of information when you call:
    *   the name of the person you want
    *   your name and your company
    *   the reason for your call

    For example:

I'd like to speak to Sarah Smith please. My name is Julia Wong from Multimedia and I need to speak to Ms. Smith about the brochure covers.

In this way the person taking the call does not have to waste time asking you questions to find out who you are and what you want.

3. Smile! Of course the person on the other end cannot see your smile. But they can hear it as you speak. A smiling voice shows warmth and is very much appreciated by the listener on the other end.

4. Do not let the other person waste time (his or hers and yours) by talking on and on about something which you did not call about. If it is you who makes the call, it is up to you to end it. You can close the conversation politely with the following examples:

I have to go now. Can I call you again if I need more information?

Thank you for your help. Now I need to go and implement your advice.

It's been nice talking to you. Thanks for your help.

5. Do not play "cat and mouse" on the phone. You call someone, he or she is not there. You leave a message to say you have called and the person calls you back. But this time you are out. You get the message and call back — your person is away again. He or she calls you back, you are out, you call back ...

This is not only exasperating, it wastes time, money and resources. To avoid this, when you call for the first time, give the person who takes your call a time frame when the person you want can call you back. As many people in Hong Kong have a mobile phone, you may leave that number so that your person may reach you at any time. Here is an example of what to say:

Please could you ask Mr. Ho to call me back between 2:30 and 4:00 this afternoon? My work number is 23456789, or he may call my mobile phone at any time. The number is 98765432. Thank you.

6. Leave full messages on answering machines. Give your name, the time and date of the call and explain why you are calling. In this way

the receiver can give you all the information you need when he or she returns the call to you. Remember, there is never any reason to rush through a message you have to leave on an answering machine.

Receiving Telephone Calls Productively

To efficiently receive telephone calls:

1. When you are on the receiving end of telephone calls, say who you are, identify your company, give a message of warmth and greeting, and, if necessary, take a message for another person. You must take messages accurately. For example:

    Multimedia Advertising, Susan Wong speaking. How can I help you?

2. If you are answering the phone for another person who cannot take the call, it is unnecessary to give details. Simply say:

    S/he's not at her/his desk at the moment. May I take a message?

3. When taking a message from a caller to pass on to another person, write the details accurately. The call could be very important, even urgent. Ask for the spelling of the person's full name, and for the contact number(s) where he or she may be reached. Spell the name back to the caller and repeat contact numbers. Note the date and the time of the call. Tell the caller that you will pass on the message.

4. If the caller asks you a question which you cannot answer and you have to put the caller through to someone who would be more in a position to give the answer, do not just say "wait a minute," and transfer the call. The caller will have no idea that a new person will be addressing him or her and such a practice is rude. Say instead:

    Please hold for a moment, I'm putting you through to Joe Lam, our senior consultant, on line 32.

    If the caller needs to call again, he or she can ask for line 32 directly.

5. Be polite and helpful at all times on the telephone. If you are the

initial contact point for your company, your telephone manner is extremely important. Rude, inefficient receptionists can cost a company money and will never be able to hold down a job for long.

Utilizing Productively Your Answering Service

If you are not available to take your calls, and have no one to take them for you, you are likely to use an automated answering system. This is generally called voice mail. Voice mail stores messages for you until you retrieve them, and can be extremely time-saving (and therefore money-saving) for a company. However unless the message is answered relatively soon, leaving a message with a machine can be frustrating for the caller. There are four ways in which you can make voice mail most productive for you:

1. If it is more usual for your callers to leave a message on your answering machine (voice mail), put this on your business card and company letterheads. By doing this people will expect to be talking to a machine and will have composed an appropriate message for you beforehand.

2. Make your greeting sound warm, helpful and friendly. Say who you are and the name of your business or company so that the caller can be assured that he or she has dialled the right number. Say you are unable to take the call and ask the caller to leave a message leaving their name and phone number, and best time for you to call back. Here is an example:

   You've reached Justin Lo of Multimedia on 29876543. I'm sorry, but I'm not near my phone right now. Please leave your reason for calling after the beep and I'll get back to you just as soon as I can. Have a great day!

3. Call your number and listen critically to your own message. How does it sound? Is it warm, helpful and friendly? Would you be encouraged to leave a message or just hang up? Is every word clear and well pronounced? If you are not happy with it, ask someone else to record the greeting for you, or you can of course use a fully automated voice-mail message. This latter, however, is never as warm and inviting as the human voice.

4. When you leave messages with machines, there is absolutely no need to rush through your message. Speak slowly and clearly. If you are giving figures, make them very clear. When leaving a contact number for yourself, slow down. It is difficult for the listener to note the number if it is rushed and will cause him or her to have to replay your message.

5. Finally, remember that good listeners and speakers are of great value to a company. Good speaking and listening skills will be a strong asset to you, from the interview process onwards. Strong speaking and listening skills are particularly required for leadership in upper management.

Exercise I

1. Why are listening and speaking skills important?
2. Name six factors which could impede listening.
3. Is it effective to take notes at the same time as listening?
4. Show how oral and written reports are similar.
5. Show how they are different.
6. Why is it important to tell listeners the outline of a speech/ presentation?
7. What makes for a good meeting?
8. What are the skills the leader of a meeting must have?
9. Name three skills of an effective participant at meetings.
10. Why is it advantageous to shine at meetings?
11. Why should a spoken report concentrate on only a few main points?
12. When answering the telephone, what three things should you mention?

Exercise II

Each student is to think about his or her own listening skills very carefully. Write down any weaknesses, as well as any strengths. It may help to think of oneself in each of the following situations:

1. Listening to a friend in a social context
2. Listening to a lecture/report
3. Listening over the telephone
4. Listening when in a meeting
5. Listening to one's boss talking to one individually
6. Listening to a recorded message

In each situation, how could you improve your listening skills?

Task I

Teacher selects one male and one female student from the class whose speaking skills are good. They are going to role-play a boss/secretary before the class. The boss is Jack Wong. The secretary is Susan Lui. Mr. Wong has just returned from a business trip. While he was away, Ms. Lui took several messages for him. These two students read clearly and at normal speed through the following dialogue while the rest of the class listens carefully to the messages that Ms. Lui has for Mr. Wong, and writes each one in note format. The two readers may pause slightly after each message.

Mr. Wong: Good morning Susan. Could I see you for a moment please?

Ms. Lui: Good morning Mr. Wong. Did you have a good trip?

Mr. Wong: Yes, thanks. Were there any messages for me when I was out of the office?

Ms Lui: Yes, several. Do you want me to go through them?

Mr. Wong: Yes please.

Ms. Lui: Okay ... Mr. Ho phoned. He said he won't be back until next week.

Mr. Wong:	Why is that?
Ms Lui:	He said he had a bad back. He's seen the doctor.
Mr. Wong:	Okay.
Ms. Lui:	Then Mr. Tung from Supercompany rang. He said he wouldn't be able to make the meeting with you on Thursday but he said he'd ring you tomorrow.
Mr. Wong:	Right.
Ms. Lui:	Miss Hwang wanted to know if she could have Thursday off. She said her sister's leaving for Canada on that day and she wants to go with her to the airport to say goodbye.
Mr. Wong:	Right. You can get through to her for me in a minute.
Ms. Lui:	And Chung's garage in Happy Valley called. They said your car wouldn't be ready for another week.
Mr. Wong:	What!
Ms. Lui:	Yes ... they're still waiting for the part from Rolls Royce.
Mr. Wong:	Well, I'll get onto them in just a minute.
Ms. Lui:	A Miss Chang called. She said she had to cancel the order for the ABL components because the customer was buying from another source instead.
Mr. Wong:	Okay. She's another one I have to call.
Ms. Lui:	Mr. Yamaha from Kyoto called. He said that he would arrive one day earlier than scheduled, on the 25th instead of the 26th. He said he would call you tomorrow.
Mr. Wong:	Okay.
Ms. Lui:	Then Rotormola Taipei called — they wanted to know if the XJS pieces were ready for shipment yet.
Mr. Wong:	Right.
Ms. Lui:	You also got a call from a woman — she wouldn't leave her name.
Mr. Wong:	Ah ... Did my wife call?

Ms. Lui: Yes, she seemed to think you would be back two days ago!

Task II

Each student is to prepare a five-minute talk on any business-related topic.

The talk is to be delivered to the rest of the class following the guidelines in "The Spoken Report." One visual aid is allowed, with three minutes for questions at the end. The rest of the class is to assess the speaker and his or her speaking skills by filling in the table below:

Criteria	Excellent	Good	Fair	Poor
Preparation				
Attention-grabber				
Indirect method used				
Slow, clear speech				
Preview of topic				
Repeats main points				
Few main points				
Transitions				
Review of topic				
Summary/conclusion				
Visual aid easily seen				
Eye contact with listeners				
Natural sounding				
Confidence				
Encourages questions				
Answers questions well				

Proofreading Exercises

Exercise I

Correct the mistakes in the following sentences.

A

1. The secretarys went out to lunch.
2. The CEO visited four main citys.
3. He also flew to five countrys.
4. The office is open until 1 p.m. on Saturday's.
5. Two attornies worked on the case.
6. The supplys will be shipped on Saturday.
7. The Wong's and the Chang's are our best customers.
8. Please reply to her faxs.
9. All office stationary is to be kept in this office.
10. How many es-mail did he send?

B

1. Was it her that phoned?
2. Me and Miss Wong visited the customer.
3. These coffee cups are she's.
4. For who was this rice box ordered?
5. Whomever is responsible for signing this invoice?
6. Every new employee must send their medical results to the head of department.
7. All of we want a bonus.
8. Only us managers will attend the seminar.
9. Only him knows how to speak Japanese.

C

1. Which product do you think is the best of the two?
2. The four managers divided the customers between theirselves.
3. Although he was newly qualified, but he worked very impressively.
4. Which do you prefer, the blue-colour or the red-colour sample?
5. He faxed a reply very quick.
6. Our new office location is much more better.
7. How much faxes will I send?
8. How many sugar do you take in your tea?
9. The new manager explains things more clearer.
10. He lied the documents on the table.

D

1. You can be sure Mr. wong that your shipment will arrive on time.
2. Mrs. Ho our senior accountant deals with all the bookkeeping.
3. We ordered a fax machine a printer an air purifyer and a photocopyer for the office.
4. Thank you for your order we received it yesterday.
5. Mr. Leung feels needless to say that the department is too wasteful of resources.
6. This month we are selling a range of tables to customers with iron legs.
7. All clocks this month are to be sold at cost to clients with glass faces.
8. I note however that only two of our sales executives will fly to Singapore.
9. June July and August are Hong Kong's hottest months.
10. We are looking forward to your continued custom Mr. Ho.

E

1. We cannot lower our prices any more this would give us too low a margin.
2. Ms. Ho will fly to Tokyo on the 28th she will meet the CEO there.
3. Our credit terms are very attractive please call us for more information.
4. A large consignment will arrive on Wednesday it will need checking.

5. Interest rates are too high borrowing money is too expensive.

6. Flying between European cities is time-saving going by rail however is more visually rewarding.

7. Small businesses rarely borrow short-term money they need however a lot of credit for production costs.

8. The tourist industry in Hong Kong is suffering with the handover out the way tourists no longer find Hong Kong an attractive place to visit.

9. Hong Kong needs to become more affordable only then will tourists visit.

10. Hong Kongs new airport will be a first for the world never before has an airport been planned on such a grand scale.

F

1. Mr. Hos two secretarys minutes will be typed up this afternoon.

2. In a weeks time we will relocate our office to central.

3. The buyers orders were received yesterday.

4. The department needs the boss approval.

5. The ladys toilets are closed due to renovation.

6. Two department's were damaged in the fire.

7. We received six fax's yesterday.

8. Please send the letter to clients home address's.

9. The taxis meter was running fast.

10. The landlord asked for three months rent in advance.

G

1. hong kong is asia's Business capital.

2. non-english speaking clients should wear headphones.

3. the title of her report was our business and the present economy.

4. chek lap kok was built to replace kai tak.

5. the ching ma bridge links lantau with kowloon.

6. The president of the company is flying in from the us next week.

7. The ceo is scheduled to arrive on thursday.

8. the currency here is the hong kong dollar.

9. The peak is an excellent place to take visiting customers.

10. The last governor of hong kong was chris patten.

Exercise II

Correct these badly written memos and letters.

1. To: Derek Chan
    From: Celia Ho, Manager
    Date: 18th April
    Subject: Sending reports from Seoul

    Hi Derek
        Dont forget to send me regular report's during your two-week
    trip to seoul i need your report's to pass onto mr. Wong. I will keep
    in touch with you by EMAIL in the meantime send anything you
    write, on the computer to me direct.

    Thanx,
    Celia

2. To: Joseph chung, head of operations
    From: Clark Lam, Manager
    Subject: Clocking-in

        I really do not see the need for employees to clock in in the
    morning's and out again in the evening's. I consider this a show of
    lack of trust in there ability to arrive and depart from work on time.
    Theirfore I propose getting rid of the clocking in/out machines
    psychologicaly, this will improove the moral of the staff i'd
    apreciate your response before the end of the week.

3. Supercompany
    118 Pine View Street
    Kowloon
    Hong Kong

    18th May 1998

    dear Mr. Woo
        Thank you for yours order of 2000 pieces of our RX11
    compoenent's wich we will deliver to you as soon as we get your

paiement please, bear in mind that we dont except credit terms from firsttime customers direct transfer in to our company acount is fine and please pay before the end of the month yours order will be delivered thereafter.

Yours Sincerely

4. mr. Jason Lec
    15/F Ketchup gardens
    whampoa
    Hongkong

Dear mr. Lee

Thanx for your inquiry about our package tours to thailand we can indeed, reserve a booking for you and your wife for the dates you require. Our Miss Chan is deeling with the hole of your booking. wed like to remind you that a 20% deeposit must be pade as soon as posible otherwise, we wont be able to reserve these dates for you and we are looking, forward to receeving yours paiement at our ofice.

yours truly

5. The Boss
    Personnel dept
    Gogetters Limited
    233 Wanchai Road
    Hong Kong

Dear Sir

Im sending my résumé to you in the hope that you will be able to find me some work in your company as you can see. I am very well qualified to do enginering work and i fel that I cood be of grate use to your firm as I herd that you are looking for mekanikal engeners at this moment and I will call you in two days to arrange a interview.

Thank you Yours sincerely

6.

Aberdeen Tartans Ltd.
56B Patterson Street
Aberdeen, Scotland

14th may 1998

Louis Chang Tailors
46–49 gift street
Kowlon
Hongong

dear Mr. Chang

    thank you for your fax. we are very pleased, that you were satisfied, with our tartans samples, but we are sory that you think that our prices quotted to you are not interesting enough we have already cut our prices for you despite the fact that ours materials qualitty is very high. If you want us to cut the price for you even more we will be forced to send to you material of leser qualitty however. As this is the 1st time that we will have serviced you and especialy since you want to place a big order, we can give you a 12 per cent discount on any order over twenty thousand hong kong dollars if you can settle, before the end of the month, we will be able to give you a further two per cent discount.

                               yours sincerely

Answers

CHAPTER 1
Exercise I (Answers vary)
Exercise II

1. Speaking, listening, reading, writing.
2. Yes, they can!
3. Makes business easier and brings business to the company.
4. Phone, fax, e-mail, voice mail, pager, letter, memo, face-to-face communication, presentation, report.
5. Their skills brings business to the company.
6. The mood of the writer, what he or she wants to say, why he or she wants to say it, and the writer's communication skills.
7. If the message is clear, if the sender knows about the subject, if the sender is in the mood to send a message, if the sender has good communication skills, if the message is sent in a calm and peaceful environment.
8. If the message is clear, if the receiver knows about the subject, if the receiver is in the mood to get the message, if the sender's communication skills are good, if the receiver gets the message in a calm and peaceful environment.
9. A message back to you from the receiver of your message.
10. By asking for feedback.
11. If the message is not clear and therefore not understood, if the outgoing message has to pass through several people, and/or if the feedback has to pass through several people.
12. Do not think that your way is the best way, do not judge, do not stereotype people.
13. Use simple sentences, ask for feedback, go slowly, step by step, apologize for misunderstandings, look for signs in the eyes that the other person is lost, listen, let the other person talk as much as or more than you.
14. Practise!
15. Know your tools, learn the techniques, have an action plan, and practise!

Task I and Task II (Answers vary)

CHAPTER 2
Exercise I (Answers vary)

A
1. He saw the customer/Mr. Yashimoto yesterday.
2. She ordered 20,000 gimlets.
3. The personnel officer/Ms. Wong said ...
4. ... 16 new Power Macintoshes ...
5. ... BMW.
6. This report from McKenzie consultants is ...
7. The Rotormola B835 order will arrive ...
8. The sales staff held ...
9. ... signed the merger agreement.
10. ... item on the agenda.

B
1. productive
2. an interesting
3. fair
4. moving
5. fair/effective/demanding etc.
6. large/small/growing/profitable etc.
7. annual
8. Microsoft XXX
9. Japanese

C
1. The supplier said that he would deliver our order of 20,000 pieces next week.
2. The sales managers held a meeting about the current month's sales to Japan.
3. Our junior managers attended a seminar for them in Hong Kong, followed by a short, in-service training.
4. The company's sales engineers will be flying to China with our sales managers for the presentation by our top executive in the field.
5. The customer has complained about our products and our sales engineers will be visiting him today to discuss another alternative.

D   (Only these answers are correct)
1. with
2. to
3. in
4. at
5. for
6. on
7. in
8. to
9. in
10. of

Exercise II (Answers vary)

A
1. flew, visit
2. confirmed
3. telephone
4. received
5. issued
6. stated
7. considered
8. spoken/delivered
9. arrived
10. return

B
1. I presented the report to the sales team.
2. I suggested a change to the boss.
3. The sales manager proposed a cut-back.
4. The customer reacted positively.
5. She suggested reducing the staff.
6. They proposed a quote to the supplier.
7. He announced that he was leaving the company.
8. He stated that the company would close.
9. He attacked his competitor in the press.
10. He witnessed the disagreement.

Task (Answers vary)

CHAPTER 3
Exercise I

A
1. Fragment
2. Sentence
3. Sentence
4. Run-on sentence
5. Fragment

B (Answers vary)
1. The sales executive ...
2. ... find their jobs stressful.
3. He slept right through ...
4. The personal assistant ...
5. We manufacture ...
6. ... are always overworked.
7. ... return from the canteen.
8. ... are always tidy.

C (Answers vary)
1. ... Engineers. They ...
2. ... city; the people ...
3. ... pieces and we ...
4. ... meeting. I took ...
5. ... morning; he seems ...

D (Answers vary)

E We are really very sorry that you found our products unsatisfactory. However, our sales engineers are confident that our new BCP components will be more compatible with your product, and we will be shipping these new pieces to you on the 17th.
   We will cover the shipping costs of both the old and these new products; we hope that you will be happy with this arrangement.

F
1. a group of sentences which develop a main idea
2. support and expand the topic sentence
3. main idea
4. sum up the paragraph or supply the last detail
5. deductive sentence organization

G
1. The secretary checked the shipment.
2. The clerk was processing the order.
3. DHL will deliver the products.
4. The Sales Manager has just praised the sales team.
5. Mr. Wong will have checked the shipment.
6. The previous manager had written the report before he left.
7. The accountant is looking at the accounts now.
8. The personal assistant lost the file.

Exercise II

A
1. We ate quickly — clause; at the restaurant — phrase
2. She filed the papers — clause; in the boss's drawer — phrase
3. The customer ordered 20,000 pieces — clause; in the afternoon — phrase
4. This morning — phrase; Mr. Lim received an urgent call — clause
5. Every so often — phrase; the secretary has a holiday — clause
6. He told the manager — clause; about the deal — phrase
7. Twenty minutes later — phrase; the plane took off — clause
8. He asked to see the boss — clause; in his office — phrase; at 2 o'clock — phrase
9. He couldn't get a flight — clause; out of China — phrase; in time — phrase
10. Don't call me — independent clause; unless it's urgent — dependent clause
11. Let me know — independent clause; if you can come — dependent clause

12. I'll do it — clause; in the morning — phrase

B There are over 70,000 merchant ships in the world. Some of these are general cargo ships. Others are specialized and are used for carrying one kind of cargo such as oil or bananas, while others may be used for passengers or holiday cruises. Because people travel mostly by air nowadays, the old passenger liners have gone out of service. However, it is still possible to travel by sea on a freighter (cargo boat) which has passenger accommodation.

C (Answers vary)
1. Your application for one month's leave has been withheld.
2. Owing to falling sales, the annual bonus for sales staff is being withheld this year.

D
1. ... and storing ...
2. ... and smoking ...
3. ... senior managers are invited to attend. All service engineers are also asked to be present.

E
1. The schedule can be changed.
2. The packages were delivered.
3. The letters are posted every morning.
4. It is being typed now.
5. It will be shipped on the 11th.
6. It was being fixed.
7. It had been sent before they called.
8. It could be done.
9. It should be sent.
10. It would be sent by Fedex.
11. It could have been done yesterday.

12. It should have been sent last week.
13. It would have been delivered last month.

F
1. It is important that Mr. Wong receives the invoice for his order number XJJ6 no later than Tuesday next week. Therefore please ask Ms. Lim to send out the invoice for order number XJJ6 to Mr. Wong before Friday.
2. Quality control is a very important part of manufacturing. It is therefore vital that our sales executives are familiar with the entire process of quality control.

G
1. This is a significant order.
2. That enabled him to save ...
3. This was unexpected.
4. These were brought ...
5. They saw different customers ...

H (Answers vary)
1. However, they saw ...
2. Therefore, he was fired.
3. For this reason, she was ...
4. On the other hand, sometimes he ...
5. Furthermore, he always ...
6. For example, she organizes ...
7. Moreover, he has complained ...

I (Answers vary)
Thank you for your order we received today. We will be shipping the products on 24th May; we confirm that you have ordered 120,000 pieces. Please note that the 25th and 26th of May are public holidays in the U.S. We will resume business on 27th May; please confirm receipt of your order after then. Thank you.

Task I (Answers vary)

Task II

A

1. Inductive — detail sentences lead up to the topic sentence which is given at the end.
2. Deductive — the topic sentence is given first, followed by the supporting detail sentences.

B (Answers vary)

C (Answers vary)

CHAPTER 4
Exercise I

A

1. So that staff can communicate with each other and therefore keep the company running.
2. Direct method states topic sentence (main idea) first, followed by detail sentences which explain/support/expand it. Indirect method puts detail sentences first, with topic sentence at the end.
3. When people write them when there is no need, or send them to many people when only one or two would benefit, etc.
4. Internal communication can use informal language, whereas communication with outsiders needs formal language. Memos are used internally and are not sent to outsiders.
5. Memos which inform, memos which request, memos which persuade. (Direct, direct, indirect, respectively).
6. Memos which inform — pleased or neutral, memos which request — pleased or neutral, memos which persuade — uninterested or displeased.
7. To, From, Date, Subject in that order.
8. It could be filed under only one subject, and the other topic could be forgotten.
9. Ask for action to be taken. Summarize the important points. End with a thought.
10. Ending suddenly is too rude and "abrupt"; need to let the reader down gently.
11. Subject, First Sentence, Body, Close.
12. This is a deadline on information requested by the writer of the memo and is followed by a reason. It gives the reader time to organize the information and lets him or her understand why he or she has to do it.
13. The direct method.

B Direct-method opening sentences are 1b, 2a, 3a, and 4a.

C

1. Subject — Intensive Sales Training Seminar
   Main idea — Intensive Sales Training Seminar on 18th March.
   Direct opening sentence — An Intensive Sales Training Seminar will be held on March the 18th.
2. Subject — Travel Discounts
   Main idea — Travel Discounts for Business Executives
   Direct opening sentence — Significant travel discounts are now available to all Business Executives through Winsome Travel.

D

1. The Regional Sales Manager will be

attending our meetings in the mornings of Monday, Tuesday, Thursday, Friday, and Saturday.

2. In order to encourage feedback on company policy, we propose the placing of suggestion boxes in several locations around the company. All employees of this company:

   - should feel free to drop a suggestion into any box at any time
   - will be given a small reward for positive suggestions
   - are welcome to make anonymous suggestions if they so wish

Exercise II

1. To: K. Mak, Training Manager
   From: S. Pang, Quality Control
   Date: 2nd February 1998
   Subject: Memo-Writing Course

   Please could you arrange for a skilled business writer to run a two-day memo-writing course for all staff in my department?

   Areas I would like covered are:
   - the two kinds of writing methods
   - uses of memos
   - characteristics of memos
   - forms of memos
   - direct-method memos
   - the memo-writing plan
   - memos that request, inform and respond

   This course can be run at any time; let me know when you have the dates. Thanks.

2. To: G. Wong
   From: A. Tan
   Date: 18th January 1998
   Subject: P. L. Lim's Travel Schedule

   Please could you give me details of P. L. Lim's trip schedule for February? I need to know:
   - the names of the customers he will visit
   - the cities/countries in which they are located
   - the dates and objectives of each visit

   If you could get this to me before this coming Friday 21st, I'd appreciate it, as I have to include this information in January's end-of-the-month report.

3. To: S. Pang, Quality Control
   From: K. Mak, Training Manager
   Date: 4th February 1998
   Subject: Memo-Writing Course

   Just to confirm that I have engaged a professional, qualified business writer, a Ms. Jane Smith, who will be pleased to run a course in memo-writing for your department staff on the 2nd and 3rd of March 1998.

   This will be a two-day intensive course, running from 9 a.m.–5 p.m. each day, in the training room.

   Let me know if I can be of any more help.

4. To: A. Tan
   From: G. Wong
   Date: 19th January 1998
   Subject: P. L. Lim's Travel Schedule
   Here is the info. you asked for re. P. L. Lim's trip schedule in February:

Date	Country	Customer	Objective
3rd	Japan	Tamagutchi	Fix parts problem
9th	Singapore	Rotormola	Meet new buyer

| 12th | Taiwan | Superco | Meet buyers |
| 16th | China | Our plant | Check Q.C. |

Let me know if you need to know anything else — happy to help.

5. To: K. Au, E. Choi, P. Lam, R. Mak, T. Pan, E. Tu

   From: G. Tse, Department Head

   Date: 3rd February 1998

   Subject: New Cost-Reduction Plan

   In keeping with the new cost-reduction plan of 25% across the company, here are details (attached) of cost-reduction activities for our own department.

   This plan is to start from tomorrow; please read the information carefully and put it attentively into practice.

   Thank you.

6. To: Quality Assurance: P. Au, C. Tam, L. Wong, J. Wu

   From: K. Choi

   Date: 21st February 1998

   Subject: Tomex Singapore Order Change

   The order for 200,000 pieces of XT3 by Tomex Singapore placed on 16th February has now been changed to 200,000 pieces of XT2.

   The reason for this change is that Tomex has reported a fault in the XT3.

   Please could you identify the fault and have it corrected before the 15th of March so that the original order for the XT3 can go ahead?

   Tomex will use the XT2 in the meantime.

   Thank you.

Task I and Task II

Obviously each piece of work must be marked on its own individual merits.

CHAPTER 5
Exercise I

A

1. If people accept your decisions, then you are likely to emerge as a leader and excel in business.

2. People do not like what is perceived to be change for the worse. Change for the better is usually liked.

3. Because it means they have to change their work habits which most people do not like to do.

4. So that when you receive sales letters, you will understand the methods the writer is using to try to get you to buy! Also you will be able to tell the difference between well-written and badly written sales letters.

5. Similar in that they are asking the reader to buy an idea. Different in that sales letters promise a product. Nothing, or very little, is offered in return in favour request letters.

B

1. Something being sold.

2. A person who can persuade others, for which he or she needs excellent communication skills.

3. Reasons are given first, by which the reader understands why action is necessary.

4. A claim is a written statement about unfair or faulty goods or services which demands remedial action. An example could be a letter to a retail store asking for a refund on a faulty

product, or a letter to a company asking for shipping fees to be reimbursed for some reason.

5. Reasons for the claim in logical order, action desired.
6. Resistance.
7. The person reading a rude or angry letter will not want to respond to it.
8. They are all written using the indirect method. They all request action and they all expect this action to be carried out.
9. You are more likely to reach a greater number of people who will actually want to buy your product.
10. You are less likely to reach a significant number of people who will want to buy your product.
11. Catching the reader's attention, stressing the selling points and reader benefits, the mention of the price, getting the reader to buy (closing the sale).
12. Appeal to the emotions if the product is inexpensive, not necessary, or will not last for a long time. Appeal to the rationale if the product is money-based (shares, insurance), if it is necessary for health or living, if it is expensive, if it will last the buyer a long time.

Exercise II

A

1. Direct method is used.
2. Tone is angry and rude.
3. Threatening legal action at this stage is unnecessary.

B

1. Direct method is used.
2. Stresses negative points for reader.

3. Is very writer-oriented, not reader-oriented.

C

1. Direct method is used.
2. Tone is rude — will not motivate staff to do as requested.
3. "Big boss" attitude — will not motivate staff to do as requested.

D

1. First paragraph offends reader — makes him or her not want to buy.
2. Works on "scare tactics" — not ethical.
3. Price is not quietly mentioned.
4. Direct method is used.

Task I and Task II (Answers vary)

CHAPTER 6
Exercise I

A

1. If the reader would feel annoyed, angry or upset.
2. Buffer, transition, explanation, bad news, alternative, closing.
3. Reduces shock. In the opening sentence(s).
4. Neutral, positive, relevant.
5. Uses an idea or words from buffer or transition to prepare for explanation.
6. Passive voice, dependent clause, long sentence, middle of paragraph in the middle of the letter, be clear without too much detail, imply the bad news, offer help
7. Do not use clichés; do not apologize; do not invite feedback; do not mention the bad news again.
8. However, unfortunately, but.
9. Beginning of letter, end of letter, beginning/end of paragraphs in the body itself.

10. In the middle of the body, in the middle of a paragraph.
11. Hurts unnecessarily. Reader may not want to continue reading the explanation.
12. When it deliberately attempts to mislead the reader.

B
1. Although the Sg876 component is no longer manufactured, we would be happy to send you a sample of the Sg877 which replaces it.
2. Although your money cannot be refunded to you without a receipt, we would be happy to give you a credit voucher.
3. Although non-company entertainment expenses will not be paid for, the company will pay for the running of company cars.

C
1. Smoking cannot be permitted in this office.
2. Credit cannot be given on this occasion.
3. Personal telephone calls cannot be made from this office.
4. Your shipment will be delayed until next month.
5. Your claim cannot be granted at this time.

D Sentences 1 and 4 are good buffers.

E (Answers vary)
Dear Mr. Nakajimo,

It was a pleasure meeting with you last week in Tokyo, and seeing for myself your excellent product line.

We are delighted that our component specifications are 100% compatible with your product GN863 range, and, although at this moment there is a small delay in production deadlines in Shenzhen, the shipment of your order at a later date is assured.

I enclose a signed waiver on shipping dues for 15% of your order, and I look forward to meeting with you again in April.

Yours sincerely

Exercise II

A (Answers vary)
Dear Mr. Lee,

It is always a pleasure to be reminded of your company's annual awards dinner.

I feel especially honoured to be asked to act as MC at this year's dinner on January the 15th; although I have another long-standing engagement on that same evening, I would be delighted to act as MC on a future occasion.

I am sure that the dinner will be a very happy and successful occasion.

Yours sincerely

B (Answers vary)
Dear Ms. Wong,

We are very pleased to be able to supply you with the products you requested, and confirm receipt of your credit application.

Although on reviewing the report from AABB Credit Information Services, terms of credit cannot be issued to you at this time, we would be delighted to work with you on a credit basis when the financial standing of your company improves.

In the meantime, a cash arrangement can easily be made. Simply order 100 items now, and enjoy a 5% cash discount. After turning over these fast-moving products, enjoy another 5% cash discount on your next order of 100 products. In this way, our products will be readily available to you and your inventory will always be complete.

We look forward to serving you soon.

Yours sincerely

C (Answers vary)

Dear Mr. Tamagotchu,

It was a pleasure to meet you at the International Trade Fair in Taipei last week where I was most interested to see your company's latest product line.

You will not be disappointed with your order of 5,000 of our GHJ components, and although a 15% cash discount cannot be given to first-time customers, we are more than delighted to discount your cash order by our 10% cash discount policy for new customers.

Your order is being processed and will be shipped this coming Monday 18th of February; we very much look forward to working with you.

Yours sincerely

Task I and Task II (Answers vary)

CHAPTER 7
Exercise I

A
1. A discussion between two sides where each tries to get what they want out of a situation.
2. Examples vary.
3. Children!
4. Without negotiation in business and trade, there is no growth.
5. Negotiation happens when the other side has what the first side wants, when the other side wants something in return. People negotiate to get

what it is they want, or at least to strike a compromise with the other side.
6. False! People negotiate only to get what they want.
7. To win, resulting in the loss of the other side.
8. A win-win situation, where both sides feel there has been compromise. So that future business with the other side can be possible.
9. Because negotiation is all about communication skills, and communication skills can be learned.
10. Being able to: (a) state what you want; (b) set your objectives inside a range; (c) summarize the objective(s); (d) form a negotiation plan; (e) put forward proposals and make offers; (f) handle offers from the other side and put forward counteroffers; (g) summarize and clarify what has already been said; (h) summarize what has already been agreed; and (i) promise future action.

B, C and D
These answers are to be assessed on their own merit.

Exercise II

There are several basic rules that these two negotiators did not follow before and during the negotiation:
1. They did not open the discussion with a clearly stated objective for the two to meet. The rep. — Mr. Chan — simply launched into an attack at Mr. Leung, and this pretty much set the tone how the discussion was going to go.
2. From the way they discussed, it did

not seem likely that either side was well prepared for this discussion. There was no negotiation plan. Each one came into the discussion with the aim that he would get the other side to agree to what he wanted, so they were not prepared to compromise. The landlord — Mr. Leung — was more calm throughout this discussion, and at one point, he did clarify a particular point said by Mr. Chan, but that was because what was said was too much of a threat, and also Mr. Leung did propose to postpone the talk to another time (promising a future action) because he felt the talk was not productive, but unfortunately the emotionally charged Mr. Chan did not take him up on this. In a negotiation, one should be, for the most part (unless emotions such as anger are part of the negotiation plan!) be emotionally disconnected from the situation such that we are not influenced by our own emotions and so that we can keep a cool head on the important issue of reaching an acceptable agreement.

3. What would strikingly obvious to an observer of this talk would be that not one of the two sides put forward any options and proposals for consideration, so no give and take was possible. In a negotiation, the more creative the negotiators are, the better; and the more options there are to consider, the easier it is for both parties to meet what they need, reaching what is called a win-win situation, where both sides feel that they have obtained something that is important and satisfactory to them. Therefore,

remember to be creative and put forward potential solutions and options for consideration. The more creative we are, the easier we would feel the negotiation go, and the better is the outcome of the negotiation. In order to be able to offer proposals, we have got to know what your bottom lines are, and this brings us back to the need for a negotiation plan.

4. The parties in the scenario were very bad at handling dialogue that go each other's way. They were not able to take one side's argument or counter-argument and develop it further for the good of both. One can see that even if only one side takes a confrontational approach, and the other side is not helping to diffuse it with more mature negotiation tactics and styles, then the talk could breakdown like it has done in this scenario.

5. There was hardly any recap throughout the talk to refocus the group and to remind both sides the purpose of the meeting.

Task I and Task II (Answers vary)

CHAPTER 8
Exercise I

A
1. Data report
2. Suggestion report
3. Reason report
4. Proposal report
5. Meeting report
6. File report
7. Precis report
8. Progress report
(Situations will vary. Teacher should mark on individual merit.)

B
1. Data report
2. Suggestion report
3. Reason report
4. Progress report
5. Proposal report
6. Meeting report — minutes
7. Precis report
8. File report
9. Progress report
10. Reason report

C   Same: They both propose a course of action to improve or remedy a situation.
Different: Reason reports are always unsolicited. Proposals are almost always solicited.

D   Same: Both are unsolicited. Both try to sell a beneficial idea.
Different: Reason reports are internal. Sales letters come from an external source.

Exercise II (Answers vary)

Task I and Task II (Answers vary)

CHAPTER 9
Exercise I

1. Formal reports are much longer; they have a standard, traditional layout, and they are not for internal reading.
2. No.
3. When management needs vital data on which to base a decision.
4. A purpose statement.
5. The direct writing style.
6. When the reader knows little or nothing about the subject, if the report is likely to upset or offend the reader.

7. First-hand and second-hand sources.
8. First-hand: interviews, company records, personal observation, surveys. Second-hand: data in libraries, newspapers, journals, reference books, computer databases.
9. The local library.
10. Time order and space order.
11. They help the reader to clearly understand the data presented.
12. Reason for writing the report, the problem, the limits of the report, the sources used, method of collecting data, main ideas, findings.
13. A summary is given if the report is simply informative. A conclusion is given when the data has been analysed.
14. States the subject of the report and who asked for it to be written. The research is described briefly and conclusions given. Gives thanks to the body who requested the report and invites feedback and discussion.
15. Your own personal thoughts and opinions.
16. The passive voice helps the report to sound more objective.

Exercise II

This work is to be assessed on its own merit.

Task I and Task II

These works are to be assessed on its own merit.

CHAPTER 10
Exercise

1. Mr. Wong agreed to ship on the 24th.

2. Ms. Kwok disagreed with the proposal.
3. Mr. Lui proposed giving a lower quote.
4. Mrs. Tu suggested deferring the decision.
5. Ms. Luk was not in favour of recruiting another secretary.
6. Mr. Choi proposed laying off two sales staff.
7. The proposal was agreed.
8. The proposal was approved.
9. The suggestion was rejected.
10. The meeting was adjourned at 10.06 a.m.

Task I and Task II (Answers vary)

Task III

Meeting of the Board of Directors of Crazy Bus Company in the Boardroom at 11:00 a.m. on Monday, 24th November 1998

Present: A, B, C, D and E
　　(Students make up their own names and titles)
In attendance:

Minutes of the last meeting were approved.

MATTERS ARISING FROM LAST MEETING
　To consider allowing drunks on buses. B disagreed with the proposal to allow drunks of the buses, and suggested instructing the drivers to drive away at top speed if a drunk tries to board a bus. The suggestion was agreed.

NEW BUSINESS
Item 1. To consider painting all buses fluorescent orange
　E and C agreed with the proposal because of the visibility this would give the fleet.

B and D were not in favour of the proposal, stating that high visibility would result in passengers having time to move to other companies' bus stops.
　It was decided not to paint the buses fluorescent orange and to continue with the same colours as before.

Item 2. To consider taking all the seats out of all buses
　As this will result in a significant increase in passengers. The proposal was agreed.

Item 3. To consider employing ex-racing car drivers for our entire fleet
　The proposition was strongly agreed in view of our most serious competitor, Deathwish Buses. A asked C to begin advertising for the fastest drivers.

Item 4. To consider a pay rise for bus drivers — how much?
　B Proposed a 400% increase from the present rate for the new drivers mentioned in Item 3.
　The proposal was agreed and approved.

ANY OTHER BUSINESS
Increase in passenger fares
　E suggested a 400% increase in bus fares to meet the higher costs of employing the new drivers (Item 3).
　The suggestion was approved.

DATE AND PLACE OF NEXT MEETING
　The next board meeting will take place on Monday, 1 December 1998 in the Boardroom at 11:00 a.m.
　Meeting adjourned at 11:45 a.m., Monday, 24th November 1998.
Signed
Dated

CHAPTER 11

Exercise I

A   Dear Mr. Lui,

The advertisement for the position of Sales Executive in the *Hong Kong News*, Friday, 18th November 1998, caught my attention.

As you will see from my résumé, since graduation I have had five years' experience in sales with GoodSales Company and I am now ready to advance to the more challenging position of Sales Executive with SuperSales Company where my experience and skills could be put to full use for the benefit of the company.

Please call me on 29876543 to arrange an interview, where I will be happy to discuss with you on a more personal level the benefits I could bring to Supersales Company.

B   Dear Mr. Lui,

I am writing to ask you if there may be an opening for me, a Sales Executive with five years' experience, in SuperSales Company.

I have been with GoodSales Company since graduating and, as you will see from my résumé, I have proven my sales abilities very well. I am now ready to offer my skills and experience for the benefit of Super-Sales, a dynamic, fast-growing company to which I feel I could make a substantial contribution.

I would like to call you this coming Monday, between 9–11 a.m., to arrange an interview where I will be better able to show you how I could be of benefit to SuperSales Company.

I look forward to meeting you.

C   Dear Mr. Lui,

Several weeks ago I applied for the position of Sales Executive, as advertised in the *Hong Kong News*, 18th November 1998.

I am still extremely interested in the position, and I would like to remind you of my experience and skills which I am certain would be of great benefit to you and SuperSales Company. Since my graduation in 1992, I have had very promising personal sales results with Good-Sales Company and I feel confident that I could bring the same achievements to SuperSales Company if I were appointed as a Sales Executive there.

I would like to telephone you this coming Monday 12th December between 9–10 a.m. when we may discuss the possibility of arranging an interview, where I would be happy to present to you how my experience and skills would benefit SuperSales Company.

D   Dear Mr. Lui,

I was disappointed to learn that I was unsuccessful in my application for the position of Sales Executive with SuperSales Company. Thank you for contacting me so promptly.

I am still very firm in my belief that my five years' experience with GoodSales Company and my undoubted sales results and skills would greatly benefit SuperSales Company if I were to be appointed as a Sales Executive with you. I am still extremely interested in a position with your company, in particular as a Sales Executive, and would be obliged if you would keep my application on file.

I would like to contact you in a month's time to discuss the possibility of an opening for me with SuperSales Company as a Sales Executive.

Exercise II (Answers vary)

Task I and Task II (Answers vary)

CHAPTER 12
Exercise I

1. We listen and speak much more than we read and write. This is also true in business.
2. Noise; illness; disinterest in the topic; concentrating on the appearance of the speaker, not the message; language problems; visual background distractions etc.
3. Yes, if the notes capture the main ideas and do not hamper the listener's concentration on the overall message.
4. Both need a plan and an outline with an introduction, a body, and a summary and conclusion.
5. Written reports usually take the direct method of communication. Oral reports most usually follow the indirect method.
6. They have nothing written to guide them. They need to know the format of what they will be hearing.
7. Ensuring that it is necessary, there are good planning, and good communication skills of the leader and the participants.

8. Strong leadership skills, strong speaking and listening skills.
9. Careful preparation, being ready to speak on an issue, knowing when to stop talking to allow others a say, being on time for the meeting!
10. Upper management will be aware of the input of productive participants, with resulting promotion if it is due.
11. Listeners cannot concentrate on more than a few main ideas.
12. Your name, your business or company, a friendly invitation to talk. (e.g., "How can I help you?")

Exercise II (Answers vary)

Task I

(Answers may vary slightly from those below.)
1. Mr. Ho. Had a bad back. Back next week.
2. Mr. Tung/Supercompany. Unable to make meeting Thurs. Ringing tomorrow.
3. Miss Hwang/Thursday off? Sister — Canada — airport.
4. Chung's garage/Happy Valley. Car one more week. Waiting part RR.
5. Miss Chang/cancelled ABL order. Customer — other source.
6. Mr. Yamaha/Kyoto. Arriving 25th not 26th. Calling tomorrow.
7. Rotormola Taipei. XJS ready to ship?
8. Woman — no name.
9. Wife — thought return two days ago.

Task II

This work is to be assessed on its own merit.

PROOFREADING EXERCISES
Exercise I

A
1. secretaries
2. cities
3. countries
4. Saturdays
5. attorneys
6. supplies
7. Wongs, Changs
8. faxes
9. stationery
10. e-mails

B
1. Was it she who ...
2. Miss Wong and I ...
3. ... are hers.
4. For whom ...
5. Whoever is ...
6. ... send his or her ...
7. All of us ...
8. Only we managers ...
9. Only he ...

C
1. ... the better of the two?
2. ... among themselves.
3. Although he was newly qualified, he worked ...
4. ... the blue or the red sample?
5. ... very quickly.
6. ... is much better.
7. How many faxes ...
8. How many sugars ...
9. ... much more clearly.
10. He laid the documents ...

D
1. ... sure, Mr. Wong, ...
2. Mrs. Ho, our senior accountant, ...
3. ... fax machine, a printer, an air purifier, and a photocopier ...
4. ... order; we received it ...
5. ... feels, needless to say, that ...
6. ... tables with iron legs to customers.
7. All clocks with glass faces are to be sold at cost to clients this month.
8. I note, however, ...
9. June, July, and August ...
10. ... custom, Mr. Ho.

E
1. ... more; this ...
2. ... the 28th; she will meet ...
3. ... attractive; please ...
4. ... Wednesday; it will ...
5. ... high; borrowing ...
6. ... time-saving; going by rail, however, is ...
7. ... money; they need, however, ...
8. ... suffering; with the handover out of the way, ...
9. ... affordable; only then ...
10. Hong Kong's ... world; never ...

F
1. Mr. Ho's two secretaries' minutes ...
2. In a week's time ... Central.
3. The buyer's ...
4. ... the boss's ...
5. The ladies' ...
6. Two departments ...
7. ... faxes ...
8. ... clients' home addresses.
9. The taxi's ...
10. ... three months' rent ...

G
1. Hong Kong ... Asia's business ...
2. Non-English speaking ...
3. The ... was, "Our Business and the Present Economy."
4. Chek Lap Kok ... Kai Tak.
5. Ching Ma Bridge ... Lantau ... Kowloon.
6. ... the U.S. ...

7. The CEO ... Thursday.   9. The Peak ...
8. The ... the Hong Kong dollar.   10. ... Hong Kong ... Chris Patten ...

Exercise II

1. To: Derek Chan
   From: Celia Ho
   Date: 18th April 1998
   Subject: Sending Reports from Seoul

   Don't forget to send me regular reports during your two-week trip to Seoul. I need your reports to pass on to Mr. Wong. I will keep in touch with you by e-mail; in the meantime, send anything you write on the computer to me directly.
   Thanks.

2. To: Joseph Chung, Head of Operations
   From: Clark Lam, Manager
   Date: 21st March 1998
   Subject: Clocking-in

   I really do not see the need for employees to clock in in the mornings and out again in the evenings. I consider this a show of lack of trust in their ability to arrive at and depart from work on time.
   Therefore, I propose getting rid of the clocking in/out machines; psychologically, this will improve the morale of the staff.
   I'd appreciate your response before Friday of this week.

3.   Fast Buck Ltd.
                                                                      118 Pine View Street
                                                                      Kowloon
                                                                      Hong Kong

                                                                      18th May 1998

   Mr. James Woo
   Senior Buyer
   Supercompany
   215 Beach Street
   Kowloon
   Hong Kong

   Dear Mr. Woo,
   Thank you for your order of 2000 pieces of our RX11 components, which we will deliver to you as soon as we receive your payment. Please bear in mind that we do not accept credit terms from first-time customers. Direct transfer into our

company account is fine. Please settle before the end of this month; your order will be delivered thereafter.

Yours sincerely

4.

GoNowhere Travel
32BB Admiralty
Hong Kong

17th March 1998

Mr. Jason Lee
15/F, Ketchup Gardens
Whampoa
Hong Kong

Dear Mr. Lee,

Thank you for your enquiry about our package tours to Thailand. We can indeed make a booking for you and your wife for the dates you require; a Miss Chan at our office will be dealing with your entire booking.

We would like to remind you that a 20% deposit must be made at the time of booking, otherwise your reservation will not be possible. We will be delighted to be of service to you and look forward to receiving your deposit and to the resulting booking of your trip.

Yours sincerely

5.

Flat B, G/Fl
118 Flower Gardens
Wan Chai
Hong Kong

25th May 1998

Ms. Chung
Head of Personnel
Gogetters Ltd.
233 Wanchai Road
Hong Kong

Dear Ms. Chung,

Enclosed with this covering letter is my résumé; a friend, Jonathan Chiew, working in your Department of Mechanical Engineering, told me that you are about to advertise for a Mechanical Engineer.

As you will see, I am well qualified in Mechanical Engineering, and I feel that I would be of significant use to your company. I will be calling you at 9 a.m. on the 27th of May to arrange an interview.

Thank you.

Yours sincerely

6.
Aberdeen Tartans Ltd.
56B Patterson Street
Aberdeen
Scotland

14th May 1998

Louis Chang Tailors
46–49 Gift Street
Kowloon
Hong Kong

Dear Mr. Chang,

Thank you for your fax. We were very pleased that you were satisfied with our tartan samples, but we are sorry that you think that our prices quoted to you are not interesting enough. We have already cut our prices for you, despite the fact that the quality of our materials is very high. If you want us to cut the price for you even more, we will be forced to send to you material of lesser quality.

However, as this is the first time that we will have serviced you, and especially since you want to place a big order, we can give you a 12% discount on any order over HK$20,000. If you can settle before the end of the month, we will be able to give you a further 2% discount.

Yours sincerely